LOSE A KILO A WEEK

The quick and effective way

NISHI GROVER

EBURY PRESS

An imprint of Penguin Random House

EBURY PRESS

USA | Canada | UK | Ireland | Australia
New Zealand | India | South Africa | China | Singapore

Ebury Press is part of the Penguin Random House group of companies whose addresses can be found at global.penguinrandomhouse.com

Published by Penguin Random House India Pvt. Ltd
4th Floor, Capital Tower 1, MG Road,
Gurugram 122 002, Haryana, India

Penguin Random House India

First published by Random House India 2012

Photographs by Vinith Bora

14 13 12 11 10 9 8 7 6

ISBN 9788184001990

Typeset in Bembo by Jojy Philip

Printed at Repro India Limited

To my parents for their immense support and love
and
my clients—every day I learn from you

Contents

Foreword

I first heard about Nishi from my niece who had been on her programme and achieved a great deal of confidence about herself from it. I was intrigued because for the longest time I had wanted to change my eating patterns and couldn't seem to find time for it in my packed schedule. It was after I joined Nishi's programme that I realized what a great nutritionist she is.

Firstly, I would like to thank Nishi for her tremendous wisdom and effort for helping not only me, but the hundreds of other women and men in whose life she's made a difference. In today's world, we all need to be healthy to stay ahead. There is huge pressure among women to look good and keep up with each other. However, our hectic schedules and the abundance that we are being endowed with are actually becoming impediments to leading a healthy and clean lifestyle. Obesity is on the rise, along with the incidence of heart disease, and just being healthy is becoming increasingly difficult to achieve.

This is where Nishi makes a difference. She is a true nutritionist, who not only helps you lose weight but also helps you maintain your ideal weight and kick start a healthy lifestyle. It's not eating less that changed my outlook towards food but eating right. And that's why she's always successful. Her mantra is simple—you are what you eat. Nishi prescribes bigger lifestyle changes rather than short cut diet plans. From her I learnt the tools of eating the right way and choosing the right foods, controlling my portions, and eating on time—the three crucial factors to controlling your weight, besides giving a great boost to your system. Her simple rule of eating with the sun—eat the most during lunch when the sun is at its peak because that's when your metabolic rate is also at its highest and cutting back in the evening, and never keeping your stomach empty made a huge difference to my life.

These, and more, simple and easily achievable ideas that she sets out are life changing and have long term benefits. Her programme makes you feel great about your body, makes you more energetic, stabilizes your mood, and keeps you as healthy as possible—all of which she teaches by a few nutrition basics and easy day-to-day dietary and lifestyle changes.

I believe that this book will be a tremendous help for people who want to make a big change in their lifestyle by making small yet crucial changes in their current habits. Packed with tips and told in Nishi's inimitable voice, *Lose a Kilo a Week* is the best gift you can give yourself.

Kavita Bhartia
New Delhi

Introduction

My journey to well-being and a healthy lifestyle was not one I had chosen on a whim. It was something I had to do. At the age of four, an age when children couldn't be bothered about the vitamins in carrots or how healthy greens are for them, I was diagnosed with Type I diabetes. And along with it came a host of other complications. While other children scampered about and ate candies and cake, I had to come to terms with the fact that my body was different—vulnerable and brittle.

Type I diabetes is extremely complex. I had to be very careful when I was growing up. Maintaining blood sugars in the normal range requires a delicate balance between the amount of available insulin and its action at the cellular level. My father, a doctor himself, taught me patience and showed me the way to combat the disease—to self-monitor blood glucose, medications and their use, exercise well and understand the importance that food plays. It was heartbreaking for him to see his little daughter unable to do things that other kids could but he saw me through some of the darkest days. I, on the other hand, didn't have a choice, and had to embrace a healthy lifestyle to battle my disease. However, I was a child and I faltered. As a teenager, I didn't comprehend the implications of not having a proper diet plan. I gave in to my impulses on many occassions—snacking at night, binging on chocolates. Of course, it was my parents who first had the enormous task of making sure I ate right and stayed healthy.

But as I grew up, and grew to understand that my body was very different from everyone else's I also understood the importance of food and exercise. Soon I made healthy lifestyle a commonplace thing and haven't deviated from it ever, well I do sometimes pop a chocolate in. I've had lapses which I have no control over but overall I am healthy, strong, and focused today because of my dedication to good eating habits and a disciplined exercise regime. So when I see people around me abuse food or eat unnecessarily, it not only makes me sad because they're throwing away their gift of having a beautifully functioning body, it also makes me angry about the wasted potential.

I embraced the concept of being nutritionally sound and physically fit and made it a part of my life. I devoured literature on health and made adjustments to my diet. This was my battle and I had every intention of fighting it tooth and nail. In 1987, I discovered aerobics and fell in love with it. It was just the sort of activity that I could be absorbed in—you work up a sweat, you breathe hard, your heart thumps keeping time with music. Aerobics was new in India, and I quickly took up a course and then began to train as a trainer. In 1988, I was certified by American Federation of Aerobics (AFA).

In 1991, I represented India in the World Aerobic championship in Las Vegas. And six months later, when Reebok opened in India, I took classes with them and soon became a certified instructor. That was just the beginning.

I was teaching aerobics three to four classes back to back. They were powerful classes, which got me and my students completely exhausted. Aerobics got me more and more into thinking about what healthy living was about. One day, a friend struggling with weight attended a class of mine and asked if aerobics could really help her lose weight. I told her that it could help her stay fit. To lose weight she first needed to eat correctly. She asked me if I could tell her what to eat and guide her a bit. I told her how I ate and about my lifestyle. She followed it religiously and, voila, she lost all her extra weight in just a few months.

My lifestyle was a successful model. It started with her, and soon the word got around. It was a gradual development, and one that was a huge learning process for me because every person's body is different and no two people have the same set of issues. I learnt something from every client who walked in through the door at Vasudevan's clinic. They all had a story of how they perceived food, what they thought about food, and why they ate. It was a long education process for me. However, over the years, I saw a pattern in my clients, and I understood what led people to eat the way they did.

The people who have come to me have all tried and dabbled in some sort of a fitness/diet/detox plan before. They are all clued into the health mantra of eating right and exercising. Yet they fail in their diets and go back to the way they usually eat. And I don't blame them because losing weight and maintaining your ideal weight is, first and foremost, about their will power—controlling the mind—a tricky thing to master. Behind every great leader, or successful person, or even religion for that matter, lies the subtle but all important disciplining of the mind. 'To enjoy good health, to bring true happiness to one's family, to bring peace to all, one must first discipline and control one's mind. If a man can control his mind, he can find the way to Enlightenment, and all wisdom and virtue will naturally come to him'—the

Buddha teaches, and there couldn't be a simpler, yet profound, truth in life.

The reason people still come to me after so many years is that I understand that they have failed before in their attempts at losing weight, I also understand the reason behind it—lack of will power and motivation. So I use a different approach when dealing with them. I don't just give them their diets and leave them to follow it on their own, because I know that will not work. In fact, I don't give them a brand new diet at all. I start with minor modifications in their current eating patterns, and gradually taper it down. This is the most flexible diet out there. If you are eating four rotis for lunch, I will make you leave one out. If you are eating dinner at 9 pm, I'll suggest you try and eat an hour earlier. If you are eating mangoes for breakfast, I'll switch them with guavas. They aren't impossible changes so most of my clients accept them happily. Then I start working on the discipline of eating and will power. However, the most important reason why the above factors work is because I chase my clients relentlessly. I insist on a daily record of what they are eating and their weight. Only when I am following up on their progress do they know that they are not in this on their own, and when they start seeing results the real journey begins because nothing is more exciting or motivating than experiencing progress first hand.

During the past several decades, food in the Western and Westernized nations has become increasingly affordable and more readily available than ever before in human history. This very fact combined with the enjoyment and stress relief that food consumption brings results in frequent overeating, which leads to a variety of chronic health problems. Today, I worry about people, especially women in India, because with the increase of incomes and affluence, Indians are eating like they never have before.

Take a look around you—fast food is everywhere. Everything is highly processed and energy dense, it's all about pizzas, sweets, chips, convenience foods, canned foods, energy drinks, soft drinks, etc. The more food is processed—through excessive cooking, pasteurization, homogenization, high heat, mechanical processing, etc.—the less natural and nutritious it becomes, to the point of becoming a harmful substance to the body, rather than a useful and nutritious element. Some industrial processing practices deprive food of their nutrients to such a high degree that the food has to be 'enriched' by artificially adding some nutrients back into it. This is especially true of flours where some vitamins are added after the processing is done.

And more than that, our palates have opened up to different cuisines. So we're not eating what we actually should be—our staple food. New foods are coming into our country, which though exotic may not necessarily be good for us. In America, heart disease is the biggest killer, topping cancer and crime, and I feel we are replicating a lifestyle which is far from ideal or healthy. Obesity is rocketing in India. I know this because the number of clients I have increases every year, and each year, the weighing scales also see bigger figures. It's a bleak scenario, and bleaker still because most people are in it with no realization whatsoever that they are killing themselves.

Why do people still come to me?

There is not one day when my clinic is quiet or my phone silent. I've been counselling and helping people lose weight for thirty years now, and my sessions are still jam-packed. My phone rings off the hook all day, with more and more people calling to join my programme. I try my best to accommodate as many as I can but it's still never enough. I think my programme works because it's simple, logical, and successful. It's also nothing drastic but a modification of your current eating patterns. It gives results and that's why people have never stopped knocking on my door. Most importantly, it hasn't ever changed because the needs of the human body will never change. The basic physiological and chemical make-up of a body requires a few basic elements to let it function smoothly and if we feed it the right things there's sure to be no hiccups. For example, you need 70 percent of carbs, 20 percent of protein, and the remaining 10 percent of sugars, fats, and minerals and vitamins. If you give your body the above in the right potrion you've done 80 percent of the job of living healthy. The rest 20 percent is good lifestyle and exercise.

My clients swear by me and keep coming back because of this particular ethic—**I show them how to eat right**. The other factor is that I'm strict and chase them till I see results. People often forget that sometimes the answers lie in the simplest things. That the food you're eating can make you fat and can also make you lose weight and bring happiness and well-being in your life. But more often than not, people lose sight of the details that make up the larger picture.

My road to healthy living has been a voyage of self-discovery. I learned that being healthy and fit can make a huge difference to one's life. It encourages mental positivity, accepting your body, gives you strength to take up new activities, and deal with any situation or roadblock that is thrown your way. More importantly, you learn how beautiful the human body can be, how kind, and forgiving of all your lapses, and you eventually learn to respect it. And that's what I want to pass on to you. I live my programme every day of my life and believe everyone can do the same. You have to be certain about what and why you need to do this.

I took it upon myself to help people relearn how to eat and give them the hope that no matter what is inflicted upon you, you can kick back to a regular and healthy system. And that's where I emphasize on a regular and frugal eating pattern for an efficient weight loss diet. When you change your eating habits permanently, when you commit to a healthier lifestyle, you eliminate all the trauma that excessive eating and random dieting bring to your life. If you're not healthy, you will never be able to give anything you do your 100 percent. With this book, I aim to bring my message about food and how working with food in the right way can make you lose weight and lead a fulfilling life. I hope this book is as beneficial to you as a reader as my programme has been for my numerous clients in India.

With that, let's get this journey to being thin and healthy started.

Before you embark this programme you must remember that in the beginning there is a lot of flexibility. You will falter but as long as you keep trying you will only get stronger and wiser watch energy little deviation. Just talk about it and take my support as you need it.

How to Use this Book

To make it simple and clear cut for easy use and unhindered reading I have divided the book into three parts.

Part I explains the issue of being overweight, its implications, understanding the causes, and learning the importance of being healthy. Being overweight is damaging us in more ways than we think and especially in India obesity is becoming a rampant illness. The rise in economic standards has made fast food more available with increased portion sizes. No longer are people eating the amounts they are supposed to be eating and this is leading to expanding waistlines and higher incidence of heart disease. People have also become more dependent on technology, making us lazier than we ever were before, and, in turn, making us move less and accumulate more fat. In this section, I also discuss emotional eating patterns and how people live in denial of their problems, waking up only when it's too late. Part I explains these causes and effects and how a regulated diet can help people lose those extra pounds. It is a crash course before we get to Part II.

Part II is a detailed, hands-on section taking you through three weeks of my diet—how to go about it and prepare for it. It has diet charts and also has a chapter for a detox diet, which you will be doing at the end of Week 2.

This section has a one-hour exercise regime that you can do in the comfort of your home. The exercise routine has been designed to complement the diet.

Part III, I feel, is the most important part of the book as it deals with that tricky problem of maintaining the weight after you've shed all the excess kilos. Here I tackle the almost impossible situation of staying at your ideal weight.

PART I

A BIG FAT ISSUE

1

'Why Am I Fat?'

'The Tendency'

It's a quarter past two. Bena is late for her counselling session. My other three clients fidget and play with their BlackBerrys to keep boredom at bay. I always start bang on time, but since this is a small group of four, I decide to wait.

Bena bursts into the room five minutes later in a swirl of Elizabeth Arden and a Hermes scarf. I grimace as she makes her way to the chair, her Aldo heels clattering across the floor. She apologizes profusely as she plops into the chair, 'So sorry, Nishi. You know how traffic is na these days. This even after I left the house fifteen minutes early. Promise, baba, won't happen again.'

I sigh, and begin the counselling session. There isn't much you can do when up against the Indian excuse of 'traffic'. But we're like that only. **We have excuses for everything**. It's the Indian defence mechanism. From the government right down to our maids, there is an excuse for every misstep. A never ending blame-game of tu-tu main-main. Take, for example, the answers to the first few questions I put forward to the group.

'Have any of you ever been on a weight loss programme before?'

'Yes,' says a young 21-year-old graduate, 'I lost 10 kg, and then I fell ill, and regained 12 kg.'

'So why do you think you put on all that weight back?' I probe.

'Don't know. Joint pains plus I have the tendency.'

There you go—'The Tendency'.

How many times have you heard women complain that they have The Tendency? That cheeky, proliferating, and inexplicable disease that seems to afflict so many Indians. I try and ask people what they mean by it. You know, try to get to the bottom of it. What, pray tell, is this 'tendency'? Does it brainwash you and tether you to the refrigerator or the cookie section of your larder that you have no control of what you're stuffing into yourself? If someone tells me they have the tendency I know that my work is cut out for me, that there lies my challenge, that this one is going to come up with a host of other excuses during the weight loss programme, and that she loves chocolate more than she likes herself. But I digress.

Bena, who is 35 years old and 40 kg overweight, has been a part of my programme before, chips in here, 'Nishi, when I got married, I was 50 kg with a waist like Priyanka Chopra's but now just look at me na... I try so hard. But even when I'm eating normally I gain weight. It's like she said...tendency meri bhi hai. Every day I check the scales lekin kya karun weight kam hi nahin hota. I just don't understand yaar...*why am I still fat?*'

I stop her there. Bena's raised a vital question. Now this is where the real session begins.

'Why Do I Put On Weight?'

Thirty years and 700 clients later it's still the same question I am asked. **'Why do I put on weight?'**

The answer is simple. What an overweight person generally does to get to their present weight is this, (provided the person doesn't have any hormonal or medical issues):

- they eat more than the required amount for their body;
- this expands the stomach to an extent where it can take in more food and increases the amount of food that can be consumed;
- they generally don't exercise, so all the food gets converted into fat rather than muscle; and

- when they go on a diet they lose a bit of weight but not enough to get them back to their original weight. So they lose hope and go back to their regular eating habits and remain overweight.

Overweight and Obesity—the Primary Culprits

The reasons why people slip into being overweight are manifold and easy to pinpoint. I have divided them into the following:

1) **Food associations**
2) **Modern-day affluence and technology**
3) **Hormonal or chemical imbalances in the body**

Let's tackle these one by one.

1) Food Associations

Bread pakore ki kasam

Most Indians are innately gracious, social creatures; we value friends and family and have a calendar filled with various holidays and occasions to celebrate, which we typically do with gusto and the biggest feature in all our festivities is, of course, food.

We Indians love our food with a fervour. We associate food with home, family, and childhood. Food can never be evil. If you're upset, your mother will probably get you a plate of sweetmeats to cheer you up. If you're stressed, you'll probably go out and get an ice cream. In one restaurant, I caught a byline 'Good food for good mood', which, I thought summed up quite articulately how we view food and what it does for us.

In India, food has this exalted place in our lives. It is sacred, to the extent that in some parts of India, the bride is given a gargantuan fish along with the rest of her trousseau. The great god Ganesha himself is often depicted holding a plate of laddoos. We show our love and affection through food. Any reason is reason enough to eat. Mums overfeed their kids; wives love to indulge their husbands; the in-laws get a kick in fattening up their daughters-in-laws; and grandparents their grandkids—a vicious cycle of feeding till we burst at our seams and find ourselves flipping through the latest issue of *Prevention* at the cardiologist's clinic. The words *'Aur lijiye'* (have some more) ring through the dining rooms of this country like a common prayer to food.

How many of us have asked 'what's for lunch?' when buttering our breakfast toast. Our days start and end with discussions about food. Most of us start planning the lunch menu at breakfast. Indian hospitality is all about eating. I go to someone's house to meet them and all they want to do is feed me. 'Arrey, Nishi, you *must* eat something,' they'll say to me in horror if I politely refuse (which I generally do). I mean, really, *must* I?

Take, for example, fasting—a common practice in many cultures. All religions have some version of fasting. Christians observe Lent—a period of forty days before Easter. It is a time of practicing self-restraint and giving up certain pleasures that one generally indulges in. People don't eat meat, fish, eggs, and especially give up something they generally like eating. In Islam, there is Ramzan when people do not eat or drink anything from dawn to after sunset. Almost one person in every Indian family goes on a Monday, Tuesday, or Thursday fast. Although the concept is religious, showing reverence to a deity, I believe that fasting in our culture originally started for purification of the system.

Fasting has many benefits. It promotes detoxification and gives the digestive system a much-needed rest. Fasting clears the skin and gives you a glow. It is a way of cleansing the self, physically, mentally and spiritually, and restoring the body's balance and even helps to reverse the ageing process. But, I feel that it serves a more important purpose—that of self restraint and controlling the mind.

However, observe a person who is on a fast today, and you'll soon notice that she/he is eating much more than they generally do on a regular day. Their tiffin will generally consist of kuttu tikkis, singhada pakodas (deep fried), potato wafers, paneer, all fruits, milk, fruit cream, sabudana. While you will probably eat just a sandwich! We love our food so much that we've even managed to turn a fast into a feast!

And if it isn't people forcing you to eat, then there's always temptation to fall back on. You go out to get your bank work done only to find that you're early and have another fifteen minutes till the bank opens. Your stomach's growling because you left in a hurry and skipped breakfast. And now you see that there's a Haldiram smack opposite the bank, and it's open. It's only normal to pop in for a bite. The day's just begun and you're already piling up on the calories.

Everywhere you go there are fast food joints, bakeries, delis, and the ever-present trap of aloo tikki, chaat, samosa, chowmein, bread pakora wallahs. If you wander out with your eyes shut you'll definitely bump into a momo guy—they're mushrooming all over the place these days. You aren't even safe at home what with home delivery bringing any whim and fancy right to your doorstep—with an extra discount. And to add to that there's your very own larder tempting you: 'C'mon step in. Eat me!' Khana hi khana, everywhere you look. It's a big bad world of food. So it's only logical that you'll end up eating more than you require, hain na?

I'm not saying that food is evil and that we should starve ourselves to death. However, today people eat more than is required for them, eat in a wrong manner, and eat all the wrong things. They've forgotten what the actual requirement is, and over eat to such an extent that it causes them more harm than anything else. Food is a beautiful thing and we can't do without it. It is our source of energy and it sustains us, gets us through our daily lives. However, we need to understand it for what it is, understand its nutritional aspects, and most of all, we need to respect it for it nourishes us and makes us healthy people. Sadly, that outlook is rapidly disappearing.

2) Modern-day Affluence and Technology

The bulge—a sign of prosperity

It is ironic that in India, a country afflicted with poverty and malnourishment, that obesity numbers are on a steep rise. And this is directly related to the economic boom that India is experiencing. The growing affluence in India has come with a heavy price—the burden of obesity.

An article by the Food and Agriculture Organization (FAO) of the United Nations calls this paradox the 'double burden'. The report 'Assessment of the Double Burden of malnutrition in Six Case Study Countries', was commissioned from national researchers in China, Egypt, India, Mexico, the

Philippines, and South Africa. 'Traditionally over-nutrition appears as under-nutrition and infectious disease become problems of the past. What we are seeing in developing countries undergoing transition is under-nutrition, over-nutrition and infections and chronic diseases coexisting over long periods of time,' says the report. The other important point the report highlighted was that given the current economic trends affecting people's lifestyle there are damaging dietary changes such as the decrease in physical activity and high salt intake, which is leading to obesity and diet related chronic diseases such diabetes and high blood pressure.

Think about it. All those growing paunches, mothers shopping for kids clothes in the adult section, women spilling out from chairs and moras. Haven't we all heard about the woman who had to book two seats on a flight because she couldn't fit into one or the one about Mr Sharma who couldn't buy the Reva because he just couldn't squeeze himself into its compact interiors? It's all true.

The thing is, India is already crazy about its food without the unnecessary business of fast food or global food. With these extra temptations, we've just made the task of staying thin and healthy that much more difficult. Ironically, the Indian diet is actually a very well-balanced one. The diets I give my patients are almost always healthier spin-offs of what their staple food is. Our plates have enough from all the food groups. Rotis or rice, a katori of veggies, some dal, and a little dahi—this is one of the most perfectly balanced meals. But today we add huge amounts of oil to ensure that our food gets cooked faster because we're always in a hurry, which then cancels out the nutritious element of the meal.

Also, all this eating out is making an impact on the kind of food that is being cooked at home. If you compare the kind of food that is cooked in a home in rural India and the food being cooked in urban India there is a huge difference. Home-cooked food today has evolved to become more masaledaar so as to keep up with our hard-to-please palates. And because we eat out so much, the food being cooked at home tastes dull and insipid. So mothers and cooks put more masala into their food to keep their children from ordering in.

A recent study led by the Organization for Economic Cooperation and Development (OECD), published in the *Lancet*—a prestigious medical journal—has ranked India in the forefront of an obesity epidemic. Between 1998 and 2005, there were 20 percent more people who were overweight or obese. One in 6 women and one in 5 men are overweight. Junk food is easy to buy for the rich but not so for the poor, which also explains why obesity knocks on the rich door.

How many of us take the elevator to the third or even the second floor? There are so many times when I'm in an elevator and I see someone press 3 that I want to say to them, 'Arre bhai, why don't you just use those things that you've dressed in trousers and shoes for a change?' I mean, really, people have stopped using their arms and legs. They're becoming redundant!

Technology is making our lives simpler, easier, and more sedentary. It is making us lazier than we ever were before. More often than not, poor dietary habits and a sedentary lifestyle are the most common contributory factors for weight gain. Look at the maids that work in our houses; they also live in today's world, but their bodies are taut and firm, and devoid of fat. That's because they put their muscles to use every day. We, the ones with access to technology, however, are doing less and less work. We are becoming a lazy bunch. All we want to do is chill. Put our feet up and do nothing. The more technology we have, the lazier we get. We're travelling more, and our palates are getting used to different cuisines. We order in, drive to the nearby market, reach for the remote, tell the servant to take the dog out for a walk, shop online. And we eat…everything…because we can now afford it. Apparently, technology and money go hand in hand with an increasing waistline. Funny na?

We all know celebrity chef Jamie Oliver and we all love his cute sa show. However, he is not just about whipping up bruschetta and making home-made tomato sauce look easy peasy. Last year, he wrote a letter to UN Secretary General Ban-Ki Moon urging the UN to put pressure on governments to support his weight loss schemes.

He wrote: '[We will soon have] a global diet of fast and processed food and drink. I have seen young mothers feeding toddlers cola through a feeding bottle because they don't understand good nutrition. One in ten people in the world is obese. It's affecting our kids—42 million are overweight before they even reach school age, and most of those beautiful children will be suffering from the early stages of heart disease and diabetes by the time they reach adulthood.'

Mothers feeding their babies Cola—imagine that!

Obesity is often confused with being overweight. The difference between them is crucial. A person can be overweight due to many factors such as muscle tone, heavier bones, etc.; however, an obese person has more body fat than he/she burns or more than the body's energy usage. An obese person generally suffers from severe and complicated health problems.

And these are just the physical problems. Apart

Obesity stops being funny when you end up with serious health complications. Some of them are:

- shorter life expectancy: obese people have a 50 to 100 percent increased risk of dying prematurely;
- diabetes (type 2);
- high blood pressure;
- heart disease;
- joint problems such as arthritis;
- breathing difficulties such as asthma;
- infertility;
- digestive disorders such as gastroesophageal reflux disease; and
- certain types of cancer (breast, uterine, colon).

Obesity is not a simple problem for it can trigger at least 53 diseases. Insulin resistance of the body can go haywire causing a major lifestyle disease—diabetes. Obesity is known to alter blood pressure, cholesterol levels, and triglycerides, all of which can trigger life-threatening health conditions.

from the above issues, being overweight/obese just makes day-to-day living so much more difficult than it need be. There is a whole gamut of social problems that arise with obesity. The issues that are most common are generally low self-esteem, underconfidence, sexual awkwardness with your partner. What's more serious is psychological problems such as depression because of negative self-image and rejection. Young Indian women who are overweight will find it difficult to find a groom, children will be embarrassed to take their mothers to school. These scenarios are becoming more and more common today.

The social implications of over eating are very dangerous. What happens is that people eat a lot, grow fat, then feel uncomfortable with their bodies, which brings on insecurity; this often leads to rejection, and ends up with the person seeking solace in more food. This is the vicious cycle of emotional eating which is very hard to break, and many end up giving up on the fight with their lives.

So why don't we put an end to it? The answer is that we all want to, but we don't because we're lazy, we have excuses, and we don't trust ourselves that we have it in us to do the job. But these are all issues which we can control. With a little bit of discipline and guidance, every one of you can beat the weight monster.

3) Hormonal or Chemical Imbalances in the Body

Despite following a low-fat diet and a strict exercise routine, a person may gain weight for other reasons which we beyond his/her control. Hormonal imbalances is one such reason.

Our body needs hormones to carry out its affairs as they are the chemical messengers of the body. However, a rise or fall in hormonal levels has repercussions on one's health and body weight. You can even be at risk of developing diabetes, infertility, hypertension, etc., due to a hormonal imbalance. Weight loss and weight gain can also be attributed to an imbalance in the levels of certain hormones. I am going to talk about the main endrocine glands and their secretions, and how they affect weight gain.

1) **Estrogen:** is a hormone that is produced in the ovaries in females. When there is a dip in estrogen levels, the body works to get the required amount of estrogen from other sources. Fat cells have the ability to synthesize this female hormone, and when there is an imbalance in the levels of estrogen, the body reacts by converting the calories into fat. Unlike muscle cells, the fat cells do not burn much calories. There is an increased accumulation of fat in your body. As a woman approaches menopause, the levels of estrogen decrease. This is the reason behind weight gain in menopausal women.

2) **Progesterone:** is another hormone that is produced by the ovaries. It helps in tackling fluid retention that may occur owing to elevated estrogen

levels. As women approach menopause, progesterone levels also decline. While body weight may increase while estrogen is synthesized from the fat cells, the body may not be able to tackle fluid retention that is caused by estrogen. Fluid retention in the body may cause one to gain weight.

3) **Testosterone:** is required for muscle building and maintenance. Muscle cells burn calories in the body and keep the rate of metabolism high. A fall in the levels of testosterone results in the loss of muscle mass. This further leads to slowing down of the metabolic rate. The final result is a gain in body weight. The level of testosterone especially declines during menopause.

4) **Androgen:** is produced by the testes in males and the ovaries and the adrenal cortex in females and is mainly responsible for the mid-section area of your body. An increase in the levels of androgen directs the deposition of fat around the abdomen.

5) **Insulin:** insulin resistance is often noticed in females approaching menopause. The side effect you suffer from is that your body converts every calorie into fat. This is one of the most obvious hormonal factors leading to weight gain in middle-aged females.

6) **Cortisol:** plays many vital roles in the body. The most important are blood pressure maintenance, fast

metabolism of fat and carbohydrates to ensure energy availability to the body, and stimulation of insulin release to maintain blood sugar. Under physiological-stress conditions, secretion of cortisone increases. This often alters the diurnal pattern of its production. This leads to weight gain. Excess fat accumulates around the abdomen, making one look bulky. The fat in the abdominal area is often called 'toxic fat' as it is strongly correlated with cardiovascular diseases like heart attack and strokes. Cortisol is often referred to as the stress hormone and explicates the relation between the stress hormones and weight gain.

Bena thinks she's eating 'normally' but she isn't. Take a look at the picture. Bena is currently at A. She's still eating more than what her body requires, and hence isn't looking thin like she wants to. When

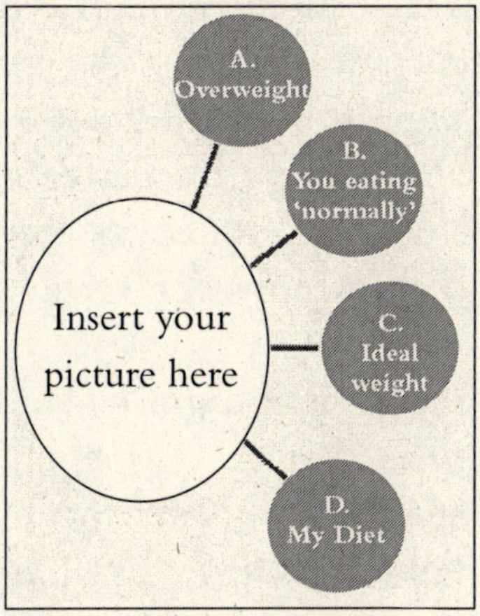

she eats 'normally' she steps down to B. But it still isn't enough to get her back to her ideal weight. What she has to do is get to D for her to be able to resume eating normally.

My Programme

Here's where I step in.

There are three phases to my programme.

Phase 1: The struggle

This is the first week of the diet where I tweak and make simple but vital changes in your regular eating pattern. The most important part I try to get people to focus on is the time they eat, that is eating more or less at the same time everyday and trying to have dinner as early as possible as much as they can. These are critical factors as they lay the groundwork for the entire programme. Eating an early and light dinner and maintaining a regular eating routine can make a world of a difference to ensuring that you lose weight quickly. However, I will go into this in another chapter.

The first week is tough because our bodies resist the changes that are being introduced. Your stomach will obviously not be too happy if it's not receiving its daily diet of the extra helpings of rice and chicken curry. It's only natural to be averse to change. This is why in this first week I try to keep the food changes to a minimum and focus on getting the rhythm and pattern of eating on the right time instead. I work on the mind. But remember human beings, as an evolutionary trait adapt to change and environments to keep up. If, in the first week, you think you can't make it, just think of how far we as a species have evolved.

Phase 2: Acceptance

By the second week, the diet gives you a few results—you will lose at least 2 kg and this will spur you on. In this phase, you'll realize that: 'I'm feeling lighter; my clothes aren't so tight anymore; I don't feel so hungry, I don't need that second helping.' This stage is pivotal in the weight loss journey.

Phase 3: Love

From Week 3 onwards, the results of the programme should encourage you to look upon the programme not as a one-time diet but as a lifelong promise to yourself to eat and feel right. You start feeling good about yourself, and, in turn, your body. Your skin will radiate, you'll have more energy in the day, and will be able to think out problems and tackle tasks with a clearer head. Every compliment you receive will push you an extra step to well being. There are two stories I would like to share about this phase. In this programme, I have something called the Deviation Day. It's the one day in two weeks when I let my clients eat anything they want—but only for one meal and that is lunch. Radha, my client, had been awaiting hers with much excitement. She had timed it perfectly so that it coincided with her husband's birthday, which I thought was very smart planning. They were going for a casual lunch in Yellow Brick Road. Before leaving she called me to ask what she should have that won't be going overboard. I told her that she could have anything she wanted as long as it was for lunch and that she compensated for it the next day.

There was a long pause at her end after which she replied, 'Nishi, it's odd. I've waited for this day so eagerly but...I don't want anything. I feel so good that I don't want to ruin it.'

The other story is about 20-year-old Maya who had just come back from the US. Her stint in the US has been devastating for her waistline, and she was determined to get back in shape immediately. She went through the first two phases without a hitch and shed all her extra kilos. When her Deviation Day arrived, she got herself a chicken burger and called me immediately after eating it.

'I'm so full I feel nauseous. I don't ever want to deviate again. Please.'

Both these women had spoken like perfect phase 3 graduates. The point is that once you see the difference in your body and understand the effort gone into getting yourself to that point, you won't feel like going back to your laidback self again.

What my programme does is give you lesser food than you're currently eating. You won't starve or faint. It will just be lesser than you're used to. Your body needs X amount of calories a day. However, you've been eating X^2 calories every day and hence are over-weight. To lose all the extra weight you can't just drop back to eating X amount of calories every day. You'll need a lesser calorie intake than that –X. Only when your intake is –X will the process of fat burning begin. My diet will give you minus X calories so that it speeds the process of fat burning, creating a deficit of calories so that you burn more calories than you consume, and eventually you will come down to your ideal or natural weight which is X. From then on all you have to do is maintain it.

This is every dietician's tried-and-tested formula, and has worked for most of my clients. Because of one factor and one factor only—RESULTS.

After all my years of practice I've found that it is only results which makes people actually go on to losing weight. And what are these results? In the first two weeks of my programme:

- you start dropping a few kilos;
- your skin starts glowing;
- your stomach goes in;
- your hair feels glossier;
- there's a spring in your step;
- you gain confidence;
- you feel motivated to take on the day and have more energy;
- your nails become stronger;
- you have a clearer mind and can tackle problems with a rational approach;
- you have better bowel movement; and
- those skintight-jeans that you loved back in the day have the possibility of an airing very soon.

Why my programme works is that my clients see results in just a week or two, and that makes a world of a difference. Nothing else will give you a boost like results.

Eighty percent of weight loss will come from a frugal diet and the remaining 20 percent is because of exercise. So diet is key. Positivity towards eating will come only from results. There is no other feeling like stepping on to your scales in the morning to discover that you have in fact, as hard as it might be to believe, lost the dreaded kilos.

And that's where my diet is bang on. You may ask now then why hasn't Bena lost her weight? Why

Madhu Trehan's (founder-editor of *India Today*) take on the diet

'Nishi's diet is effective. She doesn't deprive you of food, so you never feel hungry. Her focus is on disciplining you, and you need the zeal and passion to keep up with it. It's an education about one's self.'

is she attending a second programme at my clinic? It's because she still hasn't understood what eating involves and is still cheating on herself.

What I'm going to get you to do is rewire your thought process. And that starts with accepting that you have a weight issue and you're going to do something about it NOW.

Notes to Self

- ✔ I am lazier than I ever was before, and technology and money have a huge part to play in it.
- ✔ I'm just heading out to the supermarket and I don't need my car keys for it.
- ✔ Obesity is a life-threatening disease...
- ✔ ...one that is preventable and can be checked and reversed.
- ✔ I put on weight and never lose it because I'm eating more than I should.

2

Relearning How to Eat

In this chapter, I am going to take you through a few basic but vital things—why you eat the way you do, acknowledgement of the issue of being overweight, learning to say no, and relearning how to eat. But before we begin, I want you to take this short quiz. It'll throw up some interesting and eye-opening results…if you're honest.

The Emotional Atyachar Quiz

Q1. Do you find yourself eating when you're not really hungry?

a) Yes

b) No

c) Occasionally

Q2. During tough times, are you prone to unhealthy behaviours (eating unhealthy food, getting less sleep, binge drinking, etc.)?
- a) Yes
- b) Very rarely
- c) Not at all

Q3. Do you have confidence in yourself?
- a) Not at all
- b) Of course
- c) Yes, but I'm not overconfident

Q4. Do you find excuses not to exercise?
- a) Yes
- b) Not at all

Q5. How many times a week do you exercise?
- a) Never
- b) Twice
- c) Four times

Q6. When the going gets rough, do you find it hard to keep yourself motivated?
- a) Yes
- b) No
- c) Occasionally

Q7. Do you eat breakfast every day?
- a) No
- b) Yes
- c) Occasionally

Q8. Have you been eating larger portions than usual?
   a) Yes
   b) No

Q9. Do you often eat more than you need to and then feel heavy and guilty?
   a) Yes
   b) No
   c) Occasionally

Q10. Do you eat at unusual times??
   a) Yes
   b) No
   c) Occasionally

If you've answered **mostly a's** you have to wake up and listen to those warning bells ring because you, my dear, are an emotional eater. And you're not even aware of it!

Sudha is 26 years old, works in a prestigious advertising firm, and generally loves her job. She is gregarious and doesn't worry too much about life. On the occasions that she has a fight with her roommate she finds solace in the kitchen and churns out dish after dish. She calls herself a foodie but she actually isn't. Sudha says, 'I like cooking, it cheers me up, and after a hard day's work it's nice to know that I can drown my sorrows in chicken and mutton.'

When I told Sudha she was an emotional eater, she didn't believe me and said that there was a big difference in being a foodie and eating because of emotional reasons. She, of course, was wrong, because her eating has got her weight up to 86 kilos.

We've all been there—finishing whole packets of chips out of boredom or eating one thing after another at the slightest hint of pressure. Emotional eating is when people use food as a way to deal with feelings instead of to satisfy hunger. It's akin to a chain smoker, who lights up one cigarette after another to keep the pressure at bay. The occasional binge may seem harmless, but emotional eating can escalate into something more serious and difficult to control if it's not checked in the initial stages.

Most people eat emotionally. They don't even realize that they're doing it till one day they step on to the scales and find out how far they've come from the healthy mark. If you get into a fight or someone is rude to you, you immediately find comfort in a tub of ice cream. And who is to blame you? Food is comforting; it is one of the only daily things that directly connect us to our childhood. However, not many of us make the connection between eating and our feelings. But understanding what drives emotional eating can help people take steps to change these patterns.

The strange thing is that emotional eating need not arise because of a negative feeling. In fact, most of us like to indulge when we're in a good mood or just got a big bonus. Eating emotionally is a learned thing. Observe how a mother gives her daughter an ice cream after a test at school. What the child will do is associate food with reward and psychologically will imbibe the reward aspect of achievement and connect it with food. We, as parents, should be careful to not reward our children with excessive junk food or sweetmeats. As it sets about a cycle that becomes very difficult to break later on in life.

How to Manage Emotional Eating?

Next time you reach for a snack, stop and check whether you are really hungry. Check to see if there's something that is bothering you.

- Is there a deadline that is looming?
- Have you been getting pressurized by your boss?
- Are you fighting with any loved ones, family, or colleagues?

If yes, you've got to tackle those issues first because that's where you're probably getting your false hunger pangs from. If you can't find what's bothering you then, do something to distract you.

Call your mother or friend and just have a chat. If you have a pet, take it out for a walk. Watch a movie. Spring clean! Anything to take your mind off it.

Most emotional eaters also don't exercise at all, and that is probably why they're eating so much in the first place. I'll repeat this over and over again, but there is no substitute to a good exercise regime. It can cure most of your devils. If you really need to put something in your mouth, make yourself a healthy snack instead of chips and coke. Have a fruit or a whole wheat cucumber sandwich.

TIP OFF

Never enter or go near your kitchen or larder if you're upset or have just had a fight with someone or even when you're extremely happy. Chances are you'll clear it out and then feel worse for eating so much. Stay far away from it—better still, go for a walk. Nothing like some fresh air to calm you down and help you stay thin.

Acknowledging the Issue of Being Overweight

The curious case of the cookie lady

Leela, 39 years old and at 85 kilos, came to me with a rather confusing scenario.

'Nishi, I don't eat a thing all day and yet my weight doesn't budge from 85! What do I do?'

Leela, it seems, drank seven cups of black coffee through the day and ate two chapattis and a bowl of veggies for dinner. I was baffled—how could she live on nothing but coffee the whole day and not faint out of sheer exhaustion, and two, how was she still overweight?

I told her I couldn't take up her case as it was beyond me. A week later, a thought popped into my brain so I hurriedly rang her to ask. 'Do you have anything with your tea?'

She replied, 'Well…two or three biscuits, yes.'

'What biscuits? Be specific.'

'Anything they bring in…those ones with nuts and other crunchy things.'

There was the culprit! One cookie has approximately anywhere between 60 to 200 calories. If Leela was eating two biscuits with every cup of coffee, and drinking seven cups of coffee a day, then she was consuming a lot of extra calories without even knowing it!

Leela is what I call a denial eater. And so are most people. When clients call me on a Monday morning, begging me to put them on my programme I know they aren't sincere about it because they've had the weekend to eat and drink to their hearts' content. Sab kha pee ke aa gaye. If they were serious they'd be at my clinic on a Friday morning.

One of the first steps to losing weight is acknowledging that you have a weight issue. **After all, you are what you eat.** It's only when you zero in on the issue will you want to take steps to battle the monster. You have to accept the fact that you are a denial eater. Or you'll remain in that state of denial till one day you wake up and discover aunty-ji arms, lack energy to go through the day, and feel bloated. The only way to do this is to accept the fact that you have an issue in the first place. One which can lead to life-threatening problems. One that you have to deal with before it's too late.

It is difficult because accepting that you have a problem is not always easy. But trust me, it's an important step—one that can get the entire journey started.

The best way to take the bull by its horns is by getting on to your weighing scales every day. When my clients come into the clinic in the morning, the first thing they do is weigh themselves. Not that they necessarily want to. It's something I insist on. So much has been said about weighing scales not being the true reflection of one's weight. But I can safely tell you that's all rubbish. Weighing scales always tell you the truth, even if it's just water weight that you are losing. Stepping on the weighing scales is the first step to understanding where you stand. It also helps you know how much you have to lose—how much of the journey is cut out for you. Avoiding the scales is like living in denial.

If you don't already have one, you need to go out and buy a weighing scale. Preferably one that's digital. And make it your best friend, because it's going to know all your secrets. But first, you have to understand what your weighing scales are trying to tell you.

Learning to Say No

I recently went to a friend's daughter's birthday party. After the cake was cut, her chirpy five-year old came bounding up to me with a piece. I, however, don't eat sweets, so I said to her, 'Darling, it's your birthday. Why don't I feed you some?'

The little girl wagged a finger at me. 'Nishi, I'm diabetic. I don't touch that stuff.'

I was amazed by this five-year-old's dedication and unwavering ability to stay off something other kids her age were going nuts about. I wondered about my clients, all grown-ups, who found it so difficult to say no. And here was a child completely kicking ass.

Saying no to people, especially to your loved ones, is a hard thing to do. Learning to say no is an art. Most people don't take kindly to a no. They might feel that you are unkind, uncaring, or selfish. It will hurt and upset them and make them feel rejected.

Imagine paying your relatives a visit and trying to say no to them when they ask you to stay for tea. It's a no-win scenario where you don't really have a say. You will be staying for tea, and what's more is that you'll end up eating everything, which will be a lot, they put out. But if you want to get thin, you've got to start saying no. The next time you're going to their house and are asked to stay, tell them that you have an appointment, or if you just can't weasel out of it, stay but make a conscious decision to maybe eat just one thing from that massive spread that is coming your way.

However, you don't always have to appear rude by doing so. The trick is to say no but then back it up with something nice. For example:

Thank you so much for the invite. I would have loved to come if I wasn't so swamped. However, what are you doing on Tuesday?

See what I just did there? I said no, but I did it with tact. Remember to say it in a way that expresses respect and courtesy, and there will never be any unpleasantness.

Relearning How to Eat

A very interesting photograph I once saw somewhere shows a group of Frenchmen, heads bowed as if in prayer, before their meal. However, they weren't praying, they were taking in the aroma arising from the food.

Eating is a graceful process. Look at a formal sit-down dinner, and the number of cutlery used is astounding. There are main plates, quarter plates, soup bowls, dessert bowls, salad bowls, wine glasses, water glasses, and I'm not even going to start with the spoons, knives, and forks. However, we've completely thrown all of it out of the window. And fast food is ensuring that this lovely tradition becomes extinct. I call fast food hands-free food. I mean, do you use a fork and knife for a burger or a takeaway pizza?

And when at home, how many people actually sit down together, even if it's not together, at the dining table to eat? Most people lounge about on a sofa, watching television or are in front of their computers, Facebooking, while they shovel food down. The food has completely faded into the background. No one is paying any attention to it—its taste, its colour, its consistency, its textures. We might as well be chewing cud!

There are a few things you need to correct before we even get down to the diet. These are lifestyle changes and believe me when I say this that they make a world of a difference.

1) Sit at the table

The first thing I want you to correct is this. I want you to sit down to eat and take your time while you're doing it. You aren't that busy that you need to eat everything in a hurry. You must eat at the table. No lounging, no slouching, or lying down. Our food needs to travel directly to the stomach and to ensure that it does, you need to sit straight.

2) Never multitask while eating

The truth is that most overweight people multitask or don't sit down while eating. Multitasking while eating is the worst thing you can do to yourself because you're not paying any attention to what's going into your mouth. What you're eating is important and you need to give it its due attention for the food to be able to work its magic on you.

See how everyone at the movies eats popcorn and slurps on Diet Coke while watching a movie. First, if you're watching a movie, do just that. It's not possible that you can't get through two and a half hours without eating. And just the same way, if you're eating, try not to watch a movie, or help your kid with their homework or reply to pending mails. Sit and relax for at least one meal in the day with your family.

Aur yeh Diet Coke ka kya matlab hai? As if Coke is healthy anyway.

3) Concentrating on your food

Take time to look at what you're eating. Look at its colour, feel the texture, savour its different flavours. Only then will eating be a complete and wholesome experience. Taking your time to eat also means you will eat slowly and eat less.

4) Chew every morsel

Those who eat slowly are less prone to gaining excess weight. Don't swallow your food in great mouthfuls. It takes 20 minutes for your stomach to send messages to your brain that it is full. If you chew your food slowly you will cover that time and not end up over eating. While a slow eater is chewing only one forkful, the faster one will deliver three of them into his mouth! Most people eat in a hurry and end up over eating. This leaves them feeling stuffed and makes them slow and sluggish. There is an old saying that you should leave the table feeling half full, and there's immense wisdom in it.

If you can make these small but significant lifestyle changes of eating correctly, half your battle of weight loss has been won. These may seem minor but they are what ensure a healthy eating pattern. And they are especially pertinent in the times we live in today, when everything is consumer driven and about quick service. Make these your golden rules and live by them, and they'll serve you well in time to come.

NOTES TO SELF

- ✔ I love food, however, I've got to stop loving it so much because it's not doing me too many favours.
- ✔ Hello, table, my new friend!
- ✔ Wow, I didn't know how many different flavours there were. All I needed to do was to concentrate on my food.
- ✔ This chewing slowly business is really working. I'm starting to eat a little less than I used to.
- ✔ I want to check my email but dinner is ready. Which one am I going to choose because I can do only one thing at a time?
- ✔ Shiny shiny cutlery!

3

The 3 Big Cs

When I first met Reena, she was 26 years old, 95 kg, self-conscious and desperate. She lived alone in Delhi and didn't socialize at all. Reena found it difficult to make friends for fear that she would be ridiculed for being over weight. Then she found her way to my clinic. I counselled her and she joined the six-month programme. She was so happy with her progress after the first programme that she came back for another session.

A year and a half later, she sits poised at 55 kg chattering on about the dress she bought for her office event. I smile, watch her skin glowing with youth and the confidence she's gained after the change. How far she's come.

The thing is, so can you.

If you want to see real change you can't just read about it. You have to get up and do it. You have to make a change in order to see the change. More importantly, you can't do it whenever it's convenient for you. Nahin. You have to be disciplined about it. You have to acknowledge that your weight is a problem that you have created for yourself, you have to make time to deal with it, and you have to work very, very hard to lose it. The sooner you take charge of the situation the better it will be.

I have no shame in admitting that I'm the strictest taskmaster you'll ever come across. (Also a reason why my success rates are so high.) In the first week of my client's diet I insist on meeting them every morning with their food diary (I will talk about this in detail later). So much so that when they bump into me in my clinic they tell me with great glee, 'Nishi, I've lost 5 kilos already! Aren't you happy?' It's almost like they want to please me. I tell them that it is *they* who should be happy, not I.

The road to success (of any kind) requires self-discipline. It's hard work and toil and patience that get us there. Not jaadu. However, it doesn't mean that there's no room to make mistakes. Everyone makes mistakes, falls behind, breaks promises, misses deadlines. After all, we're only human. But the important thing is to be able to get up after the fall, dust yourself off, and continue on your journey.

The other factor that the diet is based on is simple mathematics. And everyone knows that you can't cheat math, and if you're one of those clever ones who think that you can fudge up the numbers, I'll be there to catch you at it. ☺ But enough baat-cheet. Let's get into the basic philosophy of my programme. The three broad ideas which you should try to work into your life are:

1. Mind control
2. Time control
3. Portion/Quantity control

1. Mind Control

Darling, it's all in your head

'Make me thin!' was Priya Singh's plea when she first came to me. At 22, 5 feet 7 inches Priya weighed 85 kg. She worked at Emporio Mall and the beautiful people she saw walk in and out all day made her feel worse about her weight. She joined the programme with a clear intention—that she had to be thin by hook or by crook. But I warned her that she couldn't cheat on my programme—no secret binging and no secret starving either.

She followed the programme and lost 12 kg in the first three months. She was so blown away by the changes in her body that she joined a second programme. This time she lost another 12. Then she suddenly got transferred to Jaipur and had to leave the programme. I always feel sad when I see my diligent clients leave. It makes me wonder if they'll keep to it or go back to their old ways.

A few months later I got a call from Priya. Her voice was brimming with excitement as she said, 'Nishi, I've done it. I'm at 50 now!' She wasn't even on my programme any more. I was stumped by her dedication to it. So I asked her how she did it. 'Darling, it's all in your head. So simple na. I just followed your principles and stuck to them.'

Kyaa baat hai.

She was disciplined and had her eyes set on her goal. She achieved it without my help. It's the perfect example of a person having control over the mind. That's a story I'm amazed by and use her as an example to all my clients who I have to fuss over and chase relentlessly. These clients just don't get it. As long as I'm chasing and scolding them they'll lose weight. But the instant I remove myself from the process they go back to their packets of baadam. Here's the other side of the story. For every Priya, there's a Roma. Roma is a stay-at-home mom, who's only activities involve instilling the fear of god into her maids and cook, an early evening catch-up with her friends for a short game of taash and, of course, the essential 'who's up to what', and a late evening stroll through

Select City. She's joined my programme for reasons of her own.

'Nishi, I want to lose weight from my thighs and bum. Radhika [her daughter] says that all her friends' moms wear tight, tight jeggings. Apparently they're all the rage. I went to Zara, so nice their collection is this time, last evening and tried a pair. But they just wouldn't fit ya! Kuch karo na, yaar.'

Losing weight is not really Roma's focus (and sadly, it might never be); she's more concerned about keeping up with the Jones's or in this case with Radhika's friends' moms.

Where there's a will...

The first step to losing serious amounts of weight, and trust me when I say it can happen, is to **change your attitude towards food**.

Your idea of 'normal eating' isn't on the same page as your body's idea of 'normal'. You have to re-understand what normal means, re-understand what your body needs, re-understand food and, most importantly, rewire your thought process. The logic is simple as pie, but it requires effort and again I reiterate, discipline. You have to modify your current eating pattern to get results. And there's nothing like results to encourage you and push you further on your way to becoming disciplined and healthy.

I can give you my principles but it's you who has to apply them. Eating ghiya and roti for three months and swinging back to binge eating is all nonsense. That is a fad and one that is bound to fail and injure your body more than help it. **What you need to focus on is a lifestyle change.** Without controlling your mind, there's not much anyone can do. I mean, you can only bring the horse to the water na.

You've heard it time and time again 'Where there's a will, there's a way.' Every change has to come with a mind that's made up. I don't mean to discourage you but think about it. Why do you work every day? Why do you go on a holiday? Why do you do anything for that matter?

The answer to the above questions is because YOU WANT TO earn money/like what you do/ love the beaches, etc., etc.

So now answer this question: **Why do you want to lose weight?**

The most common answer that I get from my clients is '**because I want to look good**. Feel better and more confident about myself.' You're reading this book because you want to change and because you love yourself. Because you know your body better than I do, and you want to break this cycle.

Today your food controls you, like Pied Piper pulling you out of your ideal self and leaving you in a zone that's dark, uncomfortable, and that could lead to severe health complications.

What you need to do is get out of your comfort eating pattern, and think seriously of the long-term effects of binge eating, your heart, and your overall health. **The first step is to mentally prepare yourself for less food.** You'll feel hungry but I'll give you the 20-minute eating rule. It's better to step into the battlefield knowing your enemy than a surprise ambush.

Control your mind and half the work is done. I mean, sahi mein, how much is the pleasure of food worth as opposed to a lifetime of a gorgeous body?

21 DAYS

Here's something to lift your spirits. Research has shown that it takes 21 days to form a habit. Which means that it also takes 21 days to break one. So if you're hooked on chocolates, or can't do without fizzy sodas and think you can never give it up but want to you're in luck. You only need to make a promise to yourself and keep the resolution for 21 days, after which the worst part will be over.

2. Time Control

There was a time when our grandparents woke up at 5 am and packed up their day by 8 pm. They, more than anyone else, understood the importance of a disciplined lifestyle. We unfortunately have forgotten those days, and it has led to many health problems. Our timetables have completely become ulta. We skip breakfast, eat junk for lunch, and then eat dinner like a king. Dinner has become our chilling time, we unwind while we eat it, chit-chatting, watching TV. Then to make things worse, we go out for a walk, and lo and behold the ice cream wallah around the bend beckons us for one small bar. There is an increasing number of women who come to me to lose weight which has developed due to hormonal issues such as thyroid and PCOS. This is absolutely lifestyle related. It is sad, but we have come so far away from the simple and frugal existence of our ancestors that all we can now do is tackle these lifestyle monsters that we have created.

I value time more than anything else. I'm rarely late, and I hate it when others are late. Time is money. Time is short. But more importantly, in this case, time can make you lose weight.

How?

Here's the thing. **Eating at the right time can solve 90 percent of your weight problems**. But in our hectic lives the focus has shifted to 'what' you eat instead of 'when' you eat. And that's why most of our weight troubles have mushroomed. Don't misunderstand me. The 'what' you eat bit is also crucial, but the trick to losing weight is the 'when'. Figure out the time riddle and you'll be the master of your body. Here's why.

The body clock

- How many days in a week do you wake up at a fixed time?
- Does your sleep break just as the first light starts filtering in through your curtains?
- When you wake up, do you feel fresh and raring to go?

If the answer to the above questions is none, no, and no again, you, my dear, are in need of some serious discipline. The body clock is one of the most important systems that govern our bodies. If it goes awry, our bodies get confused and start to malfunction. If you're used to waking up without using an alarm, then your body clock is functioning properly.

Light and darkness, or day and night, govern the human body more than you think they do. The **circadian system is a person's internal biological clock that regulates a variety of biological**

processes according to an approximate 24-hour period. The body systems with the most prominent circadian variations are the sleep–wake cycle, the temperature regulation system, **digestive secretions**, and the endocrine system. The sleep–wake cycle in human beings is dependent on light and temperature. **In other words, the sun is the alarm clock for your body**. And your body clock has everything to do with your digestive system and your metabolic rate. They go hand in hand.

Very logically what this would mean is that we're supposed to wake with the sun and sleep when it sets. And likewise we've got to eat according to the journey of the sun. This translates into waking up at a reasonable time in the morning—at least 3 hours before lunch. From sunrise to noon, your metabolic rate is as its highest, so whatever you eat during this time will burn out easily. As evening approaches, your metablic rate slows down, and so should you with your food because these calories will be harder to burn.

Unfortunately most people are doing the opposite. So if you're skipping breakfast and eating a very healthy dinner at 10 pm, it makes no difference to your body. Kuch faida hi nahin. Because you're not following your body's real timetable. This is what your ideal body clock and digestive system scenario should be.

Eating with the sun

- **5-6 am**: As the sun rises, so does your body. It wakes and gets the internal organs ready for the day ahead.

- **8–8:30 am**: This is the time when your body burns a lot of calories (meaning that your metablic rate is working fast) and you need to feed it. And it calls for a big meal. This is a meal that should give you enough energy to sustain you till noon, so lots of good carbs is required. **Breakfast is the most crucial meal as it sets the tone for the day.** But sadly it's the most neglected meal because we're all rushing off to work, sending the kids off to school, or just being lazy and sleeping in.

  Whatever you do, don't starve yourself during this time. Break the fast that your body has been on since your last meal and eat now. Or your body will go into survival mode and think it's being deprived of energy, holding on to its fat reserves. It is a basic survival response. Also, food is your body's fuel just like petrol is to your car. If you deprive it of it's fuel, especially break fast, you will feel weak, sluggish, and easily tired. Remember the simple and basic law of economics—shortage leads to storage, which means that if there's a shortage of any commodity in the market, the inevitable outcome will be to hold on to or hoard your reserves. Do a survey yourself. You'll find that most overweight people miss this meal.

If you think about it, this is the one meal which is actually easiest to eat as you can have it at home before leaving for school, college, or work. All you need is a bit of planning.

- **Noon–12:30 pm**:The sun is now at its height as is the body's metabolic rate.This is when it needs the most energy because by now your body has done the maximum amount of work and is tired.This is the meal that your body *wants*.This is also the time when your body burns the most calories.

  You need energizing food, carbs again (which your body will burn quickly), and also food that is high in fibre. Chapattis are the best example of high fibrous food.

- **6–7 pm**:The sun sets, your metabolic rate is slow, and your body wraps up the burning process. During this time of the day, the body's juices start the process of absorption and assimilation, and prepares for the elimination process for the following morning. Your body is not ready to accept any more food after sunset, as it is shutting shop itself. Whatever you eat now will sink like a rock to the bottom of your stomach and turn toxic. So you need to go cold turkey after sunset.

The food–time pyramid

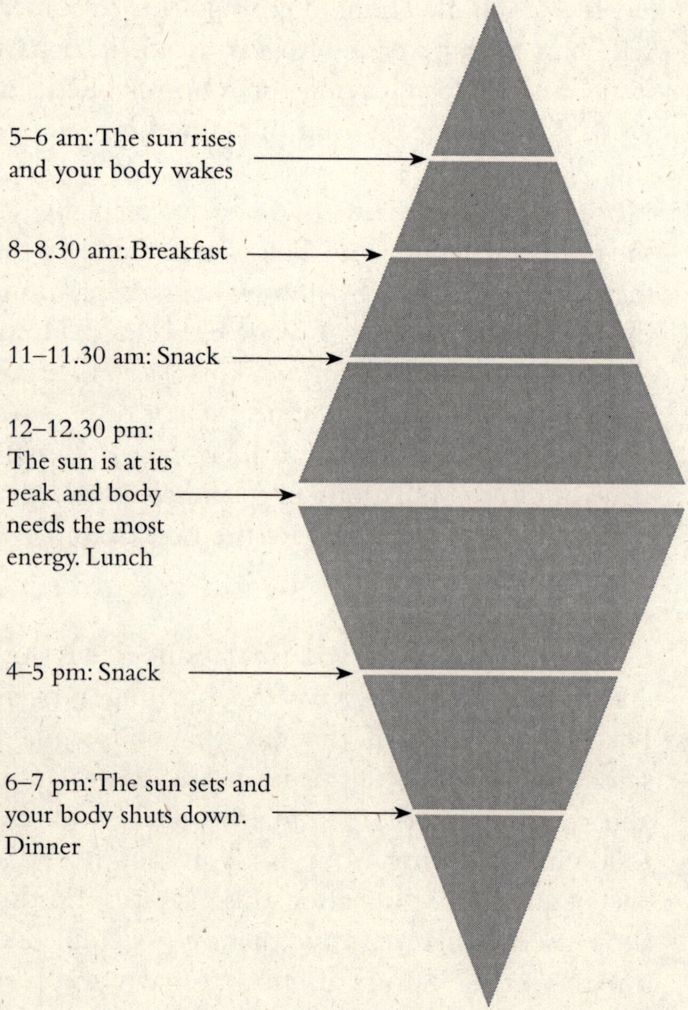

Dinner has to be a beggar's meal—lo-calorie, lo-carb, lo-quantity (CCQ). But more on that later.

The pyramid illustrates the ideal time for when we should be eating.

You can retain your body and the human body will take not more than a week to readjust and the feel good factor keeps you going.

3. Portion Control

In other words **intelligent eating**. Portion control is all about knowing how much will satiate you and how much energy you need. And it's the key to long-term weight management. Moderation is the crucial word here. If you eat in moderation you will never put on weight in the first place.

Currently, your portions are according to how hungry you are. The larger your portions the more you stretch your stomach and increase the amount of food that you can take in. Most people over eat at almost every meal. Whether it's losing weight or just plain eating healthy, your success will often depend on portion control, which will happen with time. You're better off eating moderate portions of all different types of foods, including a few treats here and there, than piling your plate up with apparently healthy options. I'm going to reverse this in a few cheeky, but strict, rules to keep your portions in check. Remember, your body will adjust to the gradual cut in portion size in time.

Rule #1: Keep your stomach half-full...always

This is every smart dieter's time-tested trick—a trick to never ever going on an all-out binge. By keeping your stomach half-full...always, you will never load your plate with anything extra, will never feel the need to binge, never end up over eating, and never put on weight. Your stomach will be happy and never crave a huge meal.

This is easily achieved by eating a piece of fruit every 20 to 30 minutes between your meals (more on this later), which are breakfast, midday snack, lunch, late afternoon snack, and finally dinner. Cut up a fruit, or ideally three different fruits, into cubes and carry them in a tiffin to office. Put an alarm on your phone 20 to 30 minutes after breakfast, and on snooze for 20 to 30 minutes after that. When your alarm goes off eat one or two pieces of fruit. Do that till your next meal. The fruit will keep your stomach full-ish and ensure that you never go all out on a meal

Rule #2: Eat slowly

You know this rule. You've heard it a thousand times. It takes your stomach 20 minutes to register that the food has arrived and for you to start feeling the effects. If you eat fast, you just end up shovelling extra, unwanted quantities of food, which will ultimately make you feel heavy, sluggish, and, of course, fat. So chew, and slowly, because this is just the beginning of your journey.

Rule #3: No second helpings

While on the programme, that is. This is a rule I adhere to come what may. The idea is to fill your plate with whatever you want in your first serving itself but to never go back for more. If your plate is visually stimulating, you'll feel satiated. So fill your plate with rotis, a sabzi, a salad, and dahi and look carefully…you have a full plate right there in front of you. This will keep you energetic and full. And of course this has to be done in tandem with Rule # 2. Which again is to chew slowly.

Rule #4: Smaller plates, bowls, cups

Yes. This means you're going shopping for new crockery. Take control of your portion sizes by downsizing your plate size. It's an easy change you can make today, and it can make weight loss way simpler. Switch from a dinner plate to a salad plate, or buy a smaller plate to use just for your own meals.

Use bowls for vegetables and spoons always. This is to ensure smaller bites and slow eating.

Using smaller dishes can also help you feel full when eating less. Studies have shown that people feel more satisfied with less food when they are served on 8-inch salad plates in place of 12-inch dinner plates. What this does is it limits the amount of food you can put on your plate but at the same time you'll also get visually satiated by your full plate of food. It's called eating through your senses. If you're eating slowly and savouring everything you're set to go.

Rule #5: The holy salad

Eat a salad 45 minutes to one hour before your big meal or if you're going out for a meal. This way you

The Four Foods That Give You Negative Calories

1. Celery: At the top of the list, celery is the king of the negative calories. One cup of celery (120 gm) contains only 19 calories. It is also an effective hydrant and an alkali, equalizing the body's PH. Celery is rich in Vitamins A, B1, B2, B6, potassium, folic acid, calcium, sodium, and essential amino acids.
2. Cucumber: High in water content (96 percent) cucumbers keep the body hydrated and cool. It also flushes out toxins. A cucumber gives you 2 to 3 calories while it takes your body 6 calories to digest it. Magic, no?
3. Lettuce: Again, lettuce is very high in water content. One cup of iceberg lettuce contains 8 calories.
4. Grapefruit: This lovely citrus fruit is high in enzymes and anti-oxidants which can reduce your cholesterol levels. However, grapefruit can have a negative reaction against a few prescription drugs. So, check with your doctor before eating it if you're on medication.

already have some food in your stomach and won't feel the need to gorge. This is a time-tested trick of not over eating. A salad has negative calories (a misnomer because all foods contain calories); what it means is that it takes more calories for your body to chew and digest it than the calories that you get from it and leave your feeling full. The best salad vegetables are cucumbers, celery, kakri, cabbage, iceberg lettuce, rocket, and asparagus. All negative calorie foods contain a lot of water too. Also raw or semi-raw veggies are rich in fibre and will fill you up. It also helps in elimination of toxins.

Now that you know the philosophy of my diet, we are going to get you ready for it.

NOTES TO SELF

- ✔ I know I have it in me to lose weight. I just need to exercise restraint and self control.
- ✔ Breakfast feels strange, but I feel more energetic after eating it.
- ✔ This keeping my stomach half-full by eating a bit of fruit every 30 minutes is really working. I don't end up gorging during lunch.
- ✔ Early dinners are great (there's none of that gas in the morning!).
- ✔ Smaller plates. Check.
- ✔ Second helpings? Never heard of such a thing in my life. ☺

4

Getting Prepped for the Diet

Why You Need to Prepare

When you go on a holiday, you don't just chuck in all your clothes into a suitcase and rush off to the airport to take the next flight out to anywhere. You plan for it.

You decide if you want to be near the sea, where it's not crowded or perhaps you feel like a bit of mountain air. Accordingly you do your research, selecting hotels and resorts of note, you mark out the dates and apply for leave, you make reservations, a list of things you will need—jackets and gloves or bikinis and beach towels. A diet needs to be approached the same way. I have had so many clients who jumped right in to the programme without really understanding the whole concept and the commitment it requires and without being mentally prepared. They eventually succeeded but it took longer. Depending on how prepared you are in your mind the time taken to settle into the diet and achieving your goals will vary. The more prepared you are the faster you will get results. A little preparation before you begin the programme will make it easier to stick with your diet for the long term and help you lose weight faster and keep it off. If you are not properly prepared before beginning, you will find it more difficult to stick with it.

There are a few things you need to do and understand before you get started. They are very basic factors which I'm sure you are already aware of but don't understand the importance. These are essential and cannot be ignored, otherwise you're not going to be knocking off any kilos. Take your time, digest it, embrace it, and then only move on to the next chapter.

Get the Green Light from Your Doc

Before you start this programme, I first want you to visit your doctor and get yourself checked for blood sugar levels, thyroid, blood pressure, and blood count. These are the basic tests to see how you are faring physically and if there are any major or minor complications. If you are overweight it is likely that you may have high blood pressure and sugar levels. So you need to track that and keep an account of it.

Set a Date

First and foremost you need to figure out a good time to start the programme. Choose your starting date carefully. Don't start your diet when you're travelling, going off on a holiday, if it's a really hectic week in the office, or there's a wedding in the family. Chances are you'll abandon it and go back on the binge. Ask yourself if it's an appropriate time and if you'll be able to devote some time to yourself, most importantly, if you will be able to make the extra effort.

Also, try starting in the beginning of a month or on a Monday. It's a mental thing, but it can give you the boost to try something new.

Mind you, time is always right when the mind is prepared.

Start Drinking More Water

You need to drink lots of water so if you're not much of a drinker, get started by carrying a bottle with you everywhere. You should be drinking at least 3 litres

Drink to Shrink

Not drinking enough water is another cause of water retention. The body holds on to water, and if you're not drinking enough water it'll hold on to whatever is already in. The old rule of economics. It's interesting to know that **you can drink water to lose weight**. You have to drink a minimum of eight glasses of water each day, or drink chamomile and jasmine tea (no caffeine or milk chai—they dehydrate you), and eat fruits.

Remember, you need 1 litre of water a day for every 10 kg that you weigh. So do the math. The more you drink, the more you'll shrink.

Also, the amount of water you drink should be the most in the morning half of your day, gradually reducing it as the day progresses. If you drink a lot of water in the evening or night, your body will hold on to it and cause water retention and a bloated feeling. So drink as much as you can during the day.

Note: No liquids 15 minutes before or after your meal.

of water in a day. If this sounds like a lot, do like I did and start adding one glass a day for a week.

Shireen, 65 years old, rang me hysterically one evening. 'Nishi, I've gained 3 kg in one day! It was 70.5 kg in the morning and now it's 73.5 kg. This is madness! And I haven't even cheated.'

I believed her. She's a diligent client and follows my diet to the T. I calmed her down and told her to ring me the next morning. True enough, the next morning she called to tell me that her weight was back to 70.1 kg. The answer to these fluctuations is water weight (along with undigested food).

Drink a bottle of water and you'll almost instantly see an immediate increase on the weighing scales. The water weight fluctuation will be on a daily basis even without changing your diet. Five hundred gm plus-minus should not alarm you. Shireen had a massive fluctuation, but even that is normal because everyone's body is different. Up to 60 percent of the human body is water (70 percent the brain is composed of water) and so weight can never be exact. There are other factors such as hormones, especially for women, and sodium retention, which can also play their part in fluctuating weight.

Exercise

Before you begin, get your body used to physical activity. If you lead a sedentary lifestyle, start doing small things which will get you moving.

Walk to the market, take the stairs, wash your own clothes. Warm your body up for the exercise that you need to do (and which is essential) when you start the programme.

Vegetables

Become familiar with vegetables on the accepted foods list (see p92) ahead of time and try several of them. This way you'll already know what you do and don't like. Trust me, you'll be eating a lot of veggies so you might as well make friends with them.

Accountability

'I'm doing everything right in your diet, but I still don't lose weight!'

This is the anguished cry I've heard from countless clients over the years.

At first, I, too, was baffled by it because the first thing I ask my clients to do is to maintain a food diary (see p65) of everything…and I mean everything…that they put in their mouth through the day. They show me this diary first thing in the morning or whenever they come to see me and I immediately know if they're deviating from the diet (food diaries can lie but the weighing scales don't) and how much weight they'll lose. The food diary is important so that I know if everything is adding up. If despite their meticulous entries they don't seem to be losing weight then, I reasoned, that there must be something that they aren't telling me. On further probing and observation I unravelled the mystery and discovered the sneaky culprit. And that, dear reader, is called nibbling.

Take this scenario for example. You go out to a party. You're not worried about the lavish spread of scrumptious lasagna, aromatic rosemary roast chicken, and the darling looking canapés that the waiter swings right under your nose because you, being smart, have already had an austere dinner at home before coming to the party. Hai na? You are, after all, following a diet and don't want to eat oily and rich party food. But as the party gears up and your friend or husband orders those canapés, one after another, you perhaps reach out and eat just *thoda sa* off their plate. Just to see how they've been made. And when dessert comes along you have just a *tiny* spoonful of kiwi ice cream from someone else's bowl, and another *small* bite of that lemon tart off another's plate.

Back home, you congratulate yourself for going through an entire party without pigging out. But what you don't realize is that you've already deviated from the programme. You've eaten more than you should have by nibbling.

Everyone does it. And what's more, people do it through the day. Your son comes up to you to open that packet of chips, and there goes a chip into *your* mouth. You're cooking in the kitchen and *you* taste a piece of mutton to check if the meat's done or *you* eat the corners of the bread while making sandwiches for your children's snack. One of my clients tells me, 'Running after my kids is like recreating *Stanley ka Dabba*. Only in this case, *I'm* the dabba!'

Nibbling is perhaps the most implicating reason why people just don't seem to let go off their pounds. That is why I emphasize that while on this programme there's going to be none of that. What I want to make clear is that all that **nibbling is unaccounted for food**.

The primary ways to be able to keep an honest account of what you're eating are maintaining a food diary and the rule of your plate and your plate only.

Your plate and your plate only

Never, ever put anything in your mouth that is not on *your* plate. You never remember unaccounted for food at the end of the day and yet you wonder why you gain weight. While maintaining your food diary you'll never remember to write about that one measly cashew or the bite of that pakoda. Every morsel has calories. So hands off other people's plates even if it's just for a tiny taste.

Your food diary

The first step to improving your diet is to increase awareness of what you eat, when you eat, and how much you eat. And there isn't a more useful tool than a food diary for it. It is a simple yet effective tool that helps you to track exactly what you eat and drink through the day. **A food diary is the best record to provide an insight into your eating patterns.** Your food diary will indicate whether your diet includes all the food groups in the amount required. The diary can throw up some startling facts about the way you eat and what you eat. It's like holding a mirror up to yourself.

When you start the programme try to maintain a food diary as deligently as possible. Just get yourself a small journal (preferably pocket size), and start. From the first day of your diet, you are going to record everything that you've eaten in a day. And I mean every morsel. It should be a simple list as below:

Time	Food	Glasses of Water
8 am	Breakfast: 2 slices of brown bread 1 cup of tea I banana	2
11 am	5 slices of cucumber	4

It will be a testimony to how well you're proceeding with eating right. The success of this exercise depends on your honesty, so no cheating. Make it a habit to jot down every time you've eaten something, when you've eaten it, and the amount. Be accurate and quick to list everything you eat. Don't rely on memory because sometimes even your memory can fail you. Once you make a habit of writing in your food diary, it'll come easy, and in the long run can help you stay on track and maintain your weight for a longer period.

Benefits of maintaining a food diary

1. Allows you to monitor your caloric intake.

2. More often than not we over eat because we are focusing on something other than what we are eating. Writing down what you eat in a food diary forces you to focus on what you are doing.

3. Encourages intelligent eating because when you record what you've eaten, you can also see where you've messed up. Think and eat. Don't eat and think.

4. It is an indicator of whether you're getting enough of each food group, and, in turn, if your diet is balanced. Your diary can tell you if you're missing out on something essential.

5. It strengthens the bond between you and your goal to get thin.

6. It helps your dietician (me in this case) tell if you're cheating when she assesses your food diary and your weight.

Clear Out the Larder

Let's start my making you poison-free. You know better than I do that guests never come unannounced, so why are you still hoarding five packets of different types of bhujia and umpteen packets of biscuits and chips? Just in case, right? However, generally no one comes over without calling first. When you do have guests, pop by the supermarket and pick up whatever you need. If you hoard all this junk, it'll be you eating them...not your guests, that much I can guarantee.

Take a day or two before you start the programme to clear out the larder (and fridge) of anything that qualifies as junk food, fast food, or anything remotely dangerous, by which I mean fattening. This doesn't mean that you have to starve your family. Just get rid of the packet and bottled food and replace them with healthier options.

Because, believe me, will power is something and 2 am hunger is another thing. If you ever wake up at 2 am and find yourself in the throes of unimaginable hunger, you're not going to have will power telling you what a good girl you've been, you're going to say, 'To hell with Nishi. To hell with the diet,' and reach for the first slice of cake. So get clearing!

Early to Bed

This is for your own good. This is a programme that ends at 6.30, latest 7 pm once you get used to the changes of eating at these times. After which you are on your own, and I hope without any food. If you're going to stay up late, you're bound to get hungry. And now that you have a larder devoid of the evil stuff, what are you going to eat when the clock strikes 12? So tuck in early.

And no driving to the nearby 24x7 for a hotdog.

Eat on Your Own

...till you have the will power to continue without getting tempted when you see food. Eating with the family is going to be one big temptation what with all the 'please pass me the potatoes, the chicken, the pasta'. I have faith in will power but if food is swung right under your nose 20 times during the course of a meal, even the devil will let you off the hook.

The best thing about this programme is that I aim to get you to eat an early dinner, and I don't think your family will take very kindly to eating so early. All the better for you, and seize this as an opportunity for you to eat undisturbed and without any temptation. **Remember, out of sight, out of mind. Mind over mouth.**

NOTES TO SELF

- ✔ Blood tests. Check.
- ✔ All other tests. Check.
- ✔ I'm ready to start.
- ✔ I take my food diary wherever I go.
- ✔ Do I want a spoon of your kiwi ice cream? No thank you, but I've already my share of the strawberry crush and it was divine.
- ✔ I've spring cleaned and detoxified my larder. Not a spot of junk food anywhere.
- ✔ I can deal with whatever it is in the morning, now I need to call it a day and get my beauty sleep.
- ✔ It's a bit quiet eating on my own but I do get to eat slowly and savour my food. Also, I don't think I can resist the chicken curry Kamla's made for the rest of the family. Not just now at least.

5

What is This Programme All About?

Cheques and Balances

'How many calories should I eat a day to lose weight?'

I am asked this by 99 percent of my clients. It's a good question. However, I always have a sneaky suspicion that they don't know what they're really talking about. A lot of people nowadays disagree with counting calories. It's apparently the wrong way to approach losing weight and is redundant. I disagree.

Reza was at 90 kg when she came to me. She told me she had tried 'everything' to lose it. She wasn't keen on going on a diet and counting calories. According to her that was 'so passe'. She wanted a diet which wouldn't stop her from eating and also help her lose weight. So she went off processed food and artificial sugars, avoided aerated drinks, exercised, switched to whole grains completely. Two months of healthy eating later, Reza stepped on to the scales. She was still at 89 kilos. Doesn't sound right, no?

I asked her to do exactly what she had been doing but this time maintain a food diary so that I knew every morsel that was going into her mouth. She did it for two weeks, and came back to me. I was very amused by the results. Reza, although she was eating completely healthy food, was eating way too much of it your helpings! How can you lose weight if you're eating four helpings of brown rice! That's when I told her about the magic of calorie counting. Reza, more than anything else, needed to keep track of the amount of 'healthy' food that was going into her system.

Healthy, fresh, lean foods *still* contain calories, and too many calories will defeat your very purpose. But recording what you take in and then counting calories allows one to get a healthy handle on what is required for fat loss while still maintaining a healthy and functioning body. It also gives you an idea as to what an ideal portion size is. Eating out occasionally is not impossible when focusing on weight loss. In fact, it becomes easier because you are now more familiar with what a real portion looks like, rather than the two or three portions you often find on the plates of your favourite restaurant. Plus, it's okay to treat yourself every now and then without it making a huge impact on your normal eating habits.

If you're overweight, I believe paying attention to **your daily numbers—total daily energy expenditure + how many calories you're consuming** (at least have a good ballpark estimate if you find weighing every food item too time consuming)—is important if you are aiming for maximum fat loss. All you need to focus on is eating right and you won't have to worry about calories.

Think of your body as a ledger (a beautiful ledger of course) that's keeping track of everything that's going in and everything that's staying out. In my experience, understanding how many healthy calories you should eat by establishing a target intake, even just as a rough guide, is crucial to successfully losing fat and maintaining body composition. This is your progress tracker. I've done this for years now, and for these many years my weight hasn't fluctuated more than 2 or 3 kilos. But remember these calories that you consume should be healthy calories.

Calorie counting does not have to be your way of life forever. Once you get down to your ideal weight and can maintain it, you'll automatically understand the infallibility of the logic. It'll come to you naturally.

CCQ

The diet that is most likely to bring you success is a portion-controlled, low healthy carbohydrate diet. However, by low-carb I mean only during dinner as I've mentioned earlier that your metabolism at its lowest at night.

Carbs are great and necessary sources of energy and will empower you while tackling your exercise programme. Plus, your will to exercise will be much greater, and your energy levels will be much higher if you maintain a healthy intake of carbs. Cutting them out will make you feel tired and constantly starved for food you can't have. A good, moderate amount of carbs will really help you burn calories and stay motivated to go to the gym. Eat good and healthy carbs at breakfast and lunch when your body requires the energy the most. **I call my diet CCQ—low cal, low carb, low quantity.**

Carbs—Your Frenemy

Carbs are that element of your nutritional needs that are the most fraught with complexities. You hate them but you can't do without them. They give you energy and are your building blocks so you can't chuck them out of the window. However, think early man, in contrast to current Western diets, the traditional diets of many pre-agricultural peoples were relatively low in carbohydrate in its **processed form**, and there was a lower incidence of obesity. Obesity is completely a modern phenomenon. Easy packaged food 'to go' has led us to eat more, eat quicker, and eat stale. Modernization altered many aspects of lifestyle, and the change in nutrition—specifically the introduction of sugar and flour—has led to many health issues. Lifestyles have changed and the body is generally under too much stress which leads to eating without thinking. So think before you eat and not eat before you think.

What I'm going to focus on in this programme is how to burn that fat with a combination of eating right and exercising. This diet is fashioned on simple mathematics. It's clear, logical, and works like a dream. **It's called a deficit calorie diet and works on cutting back the number of calories you consume in a day by a bit.** The diet gives you marginally lesser calories but not cutting out on essential nutrients like carbs, protiens, vitamins, minerals, fibre and water lesser calories than you require in a day thereby burning your body's fat reserves to give you the required energy instead of it coming from food.

There are 3,500 calories in one pound (0.45 kilo, that is almost half a kilo) of body fat. The rule of thumb of my diet is creating an 'energy deficit' of 3,500 calories (equivalent to 1 pound of fat) in order to lose half a kilo.

So to lose one kilo in one week, you are going to focus on creating a deficit of 1000 calories a day, which over the course of one week accumulate and will result in one kilo of weight loss (1,000 calories × 7 days = 7,000 calories) at the end of the week. Of course, the 1,000 calories are not going to be cut out from food alone. It will be a combination of deficit calories and exercise. If you cannot exercise in a gym because of some health issues, first do what suits you, like walking and yoga.

The idea behind the diet is to cut down on the food you're currently eating from a lot to a little lesser. Currently, after eating you feel full, lethargic, and your stomach is distended. Basically, pet ko bharpoor khana mila. A stomach is like a well and you've stuffed it to the brim like a gubbara.

The mind–stomach connection takes 20 minutes. So it takes 20 minutes for your brain to register that you are full. What you generally do is overstuff your self in those 20 minutes. What you need to try to do is stop eating when your stomach is half full.

TEST

You should be able to pull your stomach all the way back to your spine after a meal. That's the sign of a healthy and properly fed stomach. Can you do it?

It's also an excellent exercise to get a flat stomach. Try it.

★ Remember that you will not be on a deficit calorie diet for the rest of your life. It's just till you get back to your natural weight. After you reach your ideal weight, all you have to do is maintain the ideal weight and resume eating but not like you were. You should keep the pattern of eating the same but with a little flexibility regarding of time and portions. The 20 minutes rule in mind.

Here's the mathematics behind how you can lose 1 kilo in a week:

Day	*Calorie Deficit (diet + exercise) (calories)*	*Accumulated Deficit (calories)*	*Kilos Lost*
1	1,000		
2	1,000	2,000	
3	1,000	3,000	

4	**1,000**	**3,500 + 500**	**Here (at 3,500 cals) you drop ½ a kilo**
5	1,000	5,000	
6	1,000	6,000	
7	**1,000**	**7,000**	**Here (at 3,500 cals) you drop 1 kilo**

I will be completely honest with you. The first three days are the most difficult, as they require staunch will power and the chances of deviating and abandoning the whole thing are high. I've seen a lot of people give up, try again, give up, try till they finally get the hang of it and then proceed smoothly. It's like kick starting a scooter, sometimes it takes a few tries to get it started. But on the 4th day, when you drop half a kilo, you will get the best encouragement to carry on. There's nothing more rewarding than seeing the results right in front of you.

So you may ask, 'Won't I feel weak if I cut down 1,000 calories a day?

The answer is no. This is a balanced diet and it gives you everything you need in terms of carbs, proteins, and natural sugars. What you will be focusing on is cutting down on excesses in your food—excess sugar, starch, refined starch, and fats. And remember, you already have a lot of stored fat in your body, so the rest of the energy will be compensated from your existing body fat. This deficit calorie diet will give you around 1,300 calories.

Exercise doubles the calorie burn out

The Other Factor

So far so good?

Unfortunately, that's just the easy part. You can go on a diet sitting at home with your feet up. However, the other half of my diet will make you get you off your sofa and get moving. Yes, I mean exercise. That indefatigable monster that rears its head at you from every lifestyle show, glossy magazine, and, of course, me. **You have to exercise to be able to shed fat. Losing weight is a synchronized combination of burning calories through exercise and creating a caloric deficit through your diet.**

Working with BMR

I've been asked this many times—'If I exercise will my fat turn into muscle?' Both fat and muscle contribute to weight. **Muscle and fat are two**

distinctly different tissues and one can't be turned into the other. Think of muscle as lead—heavy, dense, and compact, and fat as a sponge—voluminous and spreading. A lean person with more muscle could weigh more on the scale than a fat person with less muscle. Muscle will always be muscle and fat will always be fat. You can burn fat and build muscle. When you 'burn fat' you are actually shrinking the size of your fat cells by using the energy that has been stored there. When someone says 'lose weight', I take it to mean 'lose fat without losing muscle'.

BMR or Basal Metabolic Rate is the rate at which your body burns calories when you're at rest. This is the minimum amount of calories that a body requires to stay alive. BMR can be responsible for burning up to 70 percent of the total calories burnt.

Your BMR decreases with age. **After you turn 20, your BMR drops about 1 percent every year.** Every year, it becomes harder to eat whatever you want and stay slim. Every year, the job of staying fit and slim becomes 1 percent harder. You've got to modify your eating accordingly as your body is slowing down. Your muscle build up is going down at the same rate and the bad news is that your fat mass goes up as your age. So you should start eating 1 percent less and exercising 1 percent more every year.

Exercise is crucial to retard ageing. Over time, you can gain muscle mass through a variety of activities including weight lifting and other forms of resistance training. If your main goal is to bulk up, you are likely to increase your muscle mass, which could increase your overall weight. The more muscle you have the easier it is to burn calories, and this eventually leads to a higher BMR. Physical exercise not only influences body weight by burning calories, it also helps raise your BMR by building extra lean tissue. Remember, overweight people take longer to burn calories. The lower your body fat percentage, the higher your BMR.

You should try to start exercising from day 1 of this programme. Exercise doesn't always mean hitting

CALCULATE YOUR BMR

Women

655 + (9.6 x weight in kilos) + (1.8 x height in cm) - (4.7 x age in years) = BMR

Men

66 + (13.7 x weight in kilos) + (5 x height in cm) - (6.8 x age in years) = BMR

the gym. You've got to find something that clicks or works for you. However, I don't include yoga and a slow walk in the park as exercise. It should be a cardiovascular activity, something that gets your heart rate up yet you shouldn't be out of breath.

I do a different form of exercise everyday. On Mondays I go cycling with my friends in Jorbagh, run on Tuesdays, on Wednesdays I do a round of aerobics and Thursdays, I go dancing. I believe that a variety of exercise routines keeps me focused and excited.

You can, of course, pick your own activity (or see p. 148 for a one-hour recommended exercise routine). I would suggest you do this with a trainer because a trainer will push you when you give up. I recommend adding about 30 minutes of that particular exercise a day to your diet to burn maximum fat. This is only to begin with. You need to take it up to an hour a day at least—build it up gradually. Be reasonable and don't overdo the exercise, build it up slowly.

6

Recommended Foods

The Fuss About a Balanced Diet

Everyone knows what a 'balanced diet' means. However, no one seems to be following it otherwise I wouldn't have the huge number of people coming to me everyday. To put it simply, eating a balanced diet means that you choose foods in the right amounts from each of the food groups. This is as important principle of a healthy diet—eating from a wide variety of foods.

A balanced diet is important because different foods make different nutritional contributions. If we only ate carbs and nothing else, we'd miss out on vitamins, minerals, and fibres which vegetables have. I always tell people that once you lose your excess weight, you can actually eat anything you want, you don't have to give up your favourite foods. As long as your overall diet is balanced and rich in nutrients and fibre, there is nothing wrong with an occasional cheeseburger.

The Food Groups

1) **Carbohydrates** are a source of energy. They include starches and sugars, however our body digests the starches and converts them into sugars.
2) **Proteins** are a source of materials for growth and repair. They are divided into complete proteins and incomplete proteins. Complete proteins can be found in milk, cheese, eggs (especially egg whites), soy beans, peanuts, fish, and poultry.
3) **Fats** also provide us with energy and contain fat soluble vitamins. They are the most energy rich of all the food groups, however excess fat can lead to digestive problems and long term health problems such as increased blood pressure and heart disease.
4) **Vitamins** are required in very small quantities to keep you healthy.
5) **Minerals** are required for healthy teeth, bones, muscles, etc.
6) **Fibre** is required to help your intestines function correctly.

However, over the years, as our food has been more and more tampered with and processed, the term balanced diet has lost meaning. Before, people used to shop locally and buy locally grown produce, so throughout the year they would eat a varied diet. Following a diet that was high in carbohydrates with some proteins and fat added was a good way to stay healthy, as this meant that you would be eating various seasonal vegetables and fruits. Processed food, mass manufacturing, and refining has changed this. A balanced diet has actually become less important over the last 50 years, and following a balanced diet alone is no longer a route to good health. However, a **balanced natural** diet is healthy. Today, we need to specify the type of carbs that we are consuming. So regular flour is not good for you because it is a simple carb whereas ragi, buckwheat and wholegrains are good because they are complex carbs.

My diet breaks down the exact requirement of carbs, minerals, and proteins that the body requires. It is a low-calorie, high-fibre diet and it's completely nutritious. It is also a well-balanced diet that includes foods from most of the food groups. There are a few things (see below) not conducive to weight loss so I am going to leave them out of the diet. This short chapter is a note on all the things that you need to stock your fridge with and everything else that are complete no nos.

What You're Not Going to Eat

1) **Fish**: No dark and oily fish such as salmon, hilsa, tuna, or mackerel as they are very fattening. You can eat them once you're off the programme but for the time being you have to stay clear off these.

2) **Chicken**: I do not recommend too much chicken as it contains a substantial amount of fat and does not agree with weight loss. If you can't do without it, then I would suggest you buy the breasts, not the legs, only and boil it thoroughly to remove all fat.

3) **Daals**: Again, I don't recommend daals as they are not conducive to weight loss. Seventy percent of daal is starch. Just look at what happens to daal when you stick it in the fridge. It congeals and a layer of white forms on the surface. That, my dears, is starch. However, if you want to gain weight then daal, rajma, channa and lobia are the things for you.

4) **Fruit**: Not too much papaya, watermelon, mangoes, litchis, chikoo, figs, or pineapples. These are very high in sugar or are generally pumped with artificial sugar (papaya is case in point). Also, remember no fruit juices.

Tip Off

Remember, it's better to eat a fruit whole than have the juice only. Whole fruit provides you with a whole lot more nutrition than fruit juice.

The edible skins are sites of important biological activity in the life of the fruit and also high in fibre. When fruits are juiced, the skin is removed, leaving the best part of the fruit out.

The pulpy part of the fruit is also a source of fibre and other nutrients. The white pulpy part of the orange is the primary source of its flavonoids (antioxidants found naturally in plants). The juicy orange-coloured sections of the orange contain most of its Vitamin C. In the processing of orange juice, the pulpy white part of the orange is removed and the flavonoids are lost.

5) **Veggies**: No potatoes, arvi, sweet potatoes, cooked beetroot, or yams. They have a high sugar content and are starchy.

6) **Probiotic yoghurt**: I do not recommend probiotic dahi as it is largely artificial. If you open the packet, you'll observe that it barely has any water in it as dahi should. Make it at home instead using skimmed milk.

7) **Daals/Pulses**: I don't recommend any beans (except sprouts) while on this programme as they are very heavy and not conducive to weight loss.

8) **Oil**: Invisible fats are present and pre-existing in everything that we eat. All food items, from dhania to potatoes to rice, have a certain percentage of fat in them. Invisible fats make up a large portion of our daily fat intake. This is a completely fat-less diet, so we are going to cut the visible fats such as refined oil, butter, ghee, cheese, etc., and rely on the invisible fats only. There will be no oil used in this diet whatsoever (but this is only till you are on the diet).

Cooking Without Oil

When I tell my clients that there will be less oil, used in the food they are going to eat in this diet, the general reaction is one of utter bafflement. 'But how can you cook without oil?' is what I'm always asked. When I tell them that it is indeed possible to do so, I'm instantly asked if I'm boiling or steaming the food. The thing is I'm doing neither of those. Remember, the good old technique of poaching? It's made in water completely.

Oil is something we can't do without. We use it for cooking everything. However, over the years, I've come to the realization that you can cook, and very well at that, without a drop of oil. All the food cooked in my clinic café is completely oil free and I've never had a complaint about it not being tasty. However, if you're used to cooking with oil, gradually taper it down reducing the quantity you use. You don't need to eat boiled and boring food to be healthy. Here's how I do it. This is just to show you how to get started.

You need a good non-stick pan. In that, put a bit of water and chuck in your onions, garlic and whatever else you want. Keep sautéing on a low flame till they are cooked. If the water dries up, you can add a little more. Then add your masalas and keep stirring to make sure that it doesn't burn. Once the masalas are cooked you can add whatever you are going to be cooking, for example, cauliflowers, carrots, etc. It's as simple as that. Cook them till tender. The trick is to keep a watchful eye and to stir frequently. Here are three delicious oil-free recipes for you to try out.

Tomato and Ambi Rasam

Serves 4 to 6 people

Ingredients:

½ kg tomatoes
1 to 2 small ambis
2 tsp daal
½ tsp mustard seeds
1 tbsp curry leaves

¼ piece ginger
2 or 3 cloves of garlic
¼ tsp hing
¼ tsp methi dana (roasted and powdered)
2 to 3 dry Kashmiri mirch
100 g drumsticks (cut into 2-inch pieces)
100 g beans
100 to 150 g pumpkin (cut into 1-inch pieces)

- Boil the tomatoes, mangoes, and daal together.
- Dry roast mustard seeds, curry leaves, methi dana, and Kashmiri mirch together. Keep aside.
- In a pan, roast the ginger, garlic, and hing together. Put 1 to 2 tsp if required.
- Add the boiled tomatoes, mangoes, and daal mixture.
- Boil and simmer for 30 to 45 minutes, stirring constantly.
- Add salt, haldi, and some dhania powder.
- If it's not sour enough, add ½ cup of tamarind water.
- Add the roasted spices and cook for some more time.
- Dry roast drumsticks, beans, and pumpkin with ground dhania dana, garlic, ginger, a pinch of salt and Kashmiri mirch.
- Turn off the heat and add roasted mustard seeds and curry leaves. Add these vegetables in the rasam.
- Heat and eat.

Clear Mixed Vegetable Soup Made in Celery Stock

1 person (250 ml)

Ingredients:

300 ml water (50 ml is extra)
4 celery stalks without leaves (roughly chopped)

¼ tsp roasted dhania seeds
A handful of dhania stem
Peppercorns
Lemongrass
Lemon rind
Freshly roasted garlic
Salt (if not stored)
Green chillies (optional)
Coriander

- Boil all the ingredients in a pan on high flame. After it comes to a boil, simmer and put a lid on it. Keep cooking for 30 minutes—no less or it will taste like dishwater.
- Strain all the liquid and you have your stock ready.
- Chop in vegetables of your choice.
- Add lemon juice and fresh peppercorns, lemongrass, lemon rind, fresh coriander, and salt (as per taste; also since this is a dinner soup it should be low in salt content).

Roasted Vegetable Kebabs

(without a binding agent like bread or flour)

Ingredients:

2 to 3 onions
3 carrots
1 small cabbage
300 to 400 g spinach leaves
200 g pumpkin
1 small cauliflower
1 pinch methi dana
1 tsp kasuri methi
Fresh dhania

Roasted cinnamon stick
Roasted cumin
Roasted dhania seeds
2 or 3 cloves of garlic (roasted and chopped)
Ginger (roasted and chopped finely)
1 to 2 small green cardamom
1 big black cardamom
1 nutmeg
1 star anise
Salt

- Grate/cut all the vegetables finely and dry roast them on low heat with a little water if required.
- Add the spices mentioned above and cook slightly. Mix well.
- Take a small ball of the mixture in your hand and gently keep rolling it to bind it with both hands.
- Place the balls on a tray in a refrigerator for 30 minutes.
- Preheat your oven at 175 degree Celsius.
- Spread an aluminum foil and place the balls on it gently.
- Take it out after 10 to 12 minutes. Place it in your hand. Gently and with some pressure flatten it and put the uncooked side back in the oven.
- Take it out when cooked and serve with raw onions and mint chutney.

Dalia

For an amount of 1 cup

Ingredients:

1 tbsp soaked daal
½ tbsp roasted dalia

1 to 2 cloves of roasted garlic
A handful of peas
½ cauliflower
1 carrot (chopped medium size)
1 to 2 onions (chopped fine)
Ginger to taste
1 bay leaf
Cumin (roasted)
1 whole Kashmiri mirch
1 to 2 cardamoms (roasted)
1 cinnamon stick
A few black peppers (roasted)
1 star anise
Turmeric
Salt to taste

- Roast the onions in a little bit of water, and then add ginger, garlic, spices, and chilies.
- Roast it till it's golden reddish brown, then add the daal that has been soaked for two hours. Stir and mix well.
- Add 1 cup of water and boil it. Add haldi and cover it. Stir occasionally till it is cooked.
- Add the pre-boiled, pre-roasted daal. Dry the daal a bit.
- Add the vegetables which have been cut and washed. Then add water according to taste, stir, add salt and then cover it.

Chocolate Tiramisu

Ingredients:

100 ml homemade paneer (made from skimmed milk)
4 pieces sugar-free dark chocolate
¼ tsp coffee

1 tsp cocoa powder
1 ½ tsp splenda
100–200ml milk
¼ tsp oat bran (for thickening)
1 drop vanilla essence
2 sugar-free Britannia oat cookies
walnuts (optional)

For the chocolate sauce:

- Mix 3 to 4 tsp of cocoa powder in a bit of milk.
- Boil 100–150 ml milk, add 2 pieces of chocolate, half a tsp of splenda, and pinch of coffee. Add oat bran mix in tsp of cold water for thickening and add it to the milk. Mix well.
- Bring to boil and add the cocoa powder mixture. Mix well and ensure that it is lump free.
- Now, turn off the heat and add a drop of vanilla essence, lemon rind, and a pinch of cinnamon powder. Keep aside.

To make the cottage cheese mix:

- Add 2 pieces of melted chocolate in the paneer. Ensure that the paneer is lump-free by putting it in the blender.
- Add coffee and cocoa. Mix well; add vanilla essence, lemon rind, and a touch of cinnamon.

To combine:

- In a serving bowl, add half of chocolate sauce, add 1 oat cookie and layer it with the cottage cheese mixture. Then layer with the rest of the chocolate sauce.
- Garnish with grated walnuts (optional).
- Chill and serve.

What You Can Eat

1) **Fruit**: I generally recommend only fresh Indian fruits, as imported fruits are pumped with sugars and chemicals. Some of the fruits which are good for you when on the diet are:

    - Granny smith green apples as they have the least calories (30 cals) or the lovely golden Shimla apples (50 cals). Other apples have around 150 cals. Kashmiri apples have around 100 cals. Red apples are also good.
    - Grapefruit or pomelo is the only fruit which gives you negative calories.
    - Kiwi (80 cals) is rich in anti oxidants.
    - Guava is my all time favourite. This Indian fruit gives you all the essential nutrients.
    - Mausambi, oranges, and small pears.
    - Home-grown strawberries and gooseberries.
    - Cherries.
    - Pears.

2) **Whole grains**: Refined grains or flours have no bran (the hard outer layer of grain which has the highest nutritional value) in them. When these foods are consumed, blood sugar levels immediately shoot up. The body produces excess

insulin to lower the blood sugar levels. If this goes on for a long time, the body keeps pumping out large quantities of insulin and usually develops insulin resistance. High fibre carbs release glucose slowly and give you bulk. Slow release of glucose ensures that you are fuller for a long time and the bulk helps you to clear bowels.

And I recommend you make whole grains a part of your life.

Remember, there is no such thing as completely whole grain bread in the market. All bread needs a bit of flour to hold it together or it'll crumble at touch.

3) **Millets**: A varied cereal crop, millets are fantastic for their high-protein, non-glutenous, low-calorie content, and immense nutritional value. In other words, if you want the nutrition from a carbohydrate without the starch of it, millets are the answer. You not only lose a lot of weight, but the nutritional benefits make it a very healthy option.

Grains to get are bajra, jowar, ragi, and nachni millets. These absorb cholesterol and help increase the secretion of bile that emulsifies fats.

How to cook bajra?

Bajra is delicious as a cooked cereal and in casseroles, breads, and stews. It can be used as a side dish or served with sautéed vegetables or with beans and also eaten as a snack or breakfast cereal. The grain mixes well with any seasoning or herbs that are commonly used in rice dishes and for interesting taste and texture variations it may be combined with quinoa and brown or red rice.

There are many cooking variations for bajra. A general guideline is to use 3 parts water and 1 part grain, add grain to boiling water, and simmer covered for approximately 30 minutes or until the water is completely absorbed. Remove from heat and let it steam, covered for another 10 minutes.

The flavour of bajra is enhanced by lightly roasting the grains in a pan before cooking; stir constantly for approximately 3 minutes or until a mild, nutty aroma is released.

STORING MILLET

The grain should be stored in tightly closed containers, preferably glass, in a cool, dry place. The flour deteriorates and becomes rancid very rapidly after it is ground, so it is best to grind the flour right before it is to be used.

4) **Egg whites**: They are an excellent source of protein. They are a complete protein, which means they have all the essential nine amino acids. Amino acids are essential as your body uses them to reconstruct protein or repair damaged tissue in your body. I recommend that you eat one for breakfast everyday.

5) **Fish**: You can eat all the white, less fatty fish like sea bas, surmai, singhara. These are an excellent source of low-fat protein.

FOODS THAT MAKE YOU LOSE WEIGHT

Curry leaves: Flush out fat and toxins, and reduce fat deposits that are stored in the body. Incorporating curry leaves into your daily diet can help you lose weight. Put 8 to 10 curry leaves into your diet daily. Chop them finely and mix them into a drink or sprinkle them over a meal.

Cabbage: Raw or cooked cabbage blocks the conversion of sugar and other carbohydrates into fat and greatly helps in weight reduction.

Garlic: is an effective fat-burning food, as it contains the sulphur compound allicin, which has anti-bacterial effects and helps reduce cholesterol and unhealthy fats.

7

FAQs

I get asked all sorts of questions from my clients. But I don't mind. Some of them throw up issues, which I've never thought of before and some just make the mind boggle. In this chapter I want to address some of the most commonly asked questions about diet and weight loss, which will hopefully put an end to the matter.

Q. If I exercise, will my fat convert into muscle?

A: No. Never.

Fat will never turn into muscle and muscle will never turn into fat. The reason is that fats and muscles are made up of completely different cell structures and they are so different that they cannot be converted to each other. The reason people think that fats convert into muscles is when they start working out because when you lift weight, run, etc., your muscles start to develop and your fat cells shrink in size because the energy in them is being used; however your fat remains where it always has been. The immediate effect of working out is that you tend to start eating healthy and less. With a lesser calorie intake, the fat store in your body decreases and you start losing the volume that is created by fat. The work out on the other hand will build muscle and you will look leaner and more toned. To most people, however, it may seem as if the fat has turned into muscle!

Q. Does eating breakfast really help you diet?

A: Yes, not because it helps you eat less during the day, but because it gives you energy and makes you a little more active during the day.

Q. If I get an oil massage, will the oil get absorbed into my skin and make me fat?

A: It's true. I have been asked that. But the answer to the question is a big NO. It is biologically impossible!

Q. When I work out, I perspire a lot. This is a good thing, right? This means I'm losing weight?

A: Wrong. Perspiration is an indication that the body temperature coming down. It acts like a thermostat of your body. How much you sweat does not necessarily reflect how hard you're working. Some people tend to sweat profusely due to heavy body weight, poor conditioning, or other factors. And everyone sweats more in hot, dry weather than in cool, humid weather or if they wear dense clothing rather than porous clothing.

Q. Can I lose weight and keep it stable without exercising? I just don't like exercising ya.

A: It is possible to lose weight and keep it off without following an exercise programme, but it is much harder to follow and rarely successful in the long term.

Q. How do I know if I am obese?

A: Obesity is defined as an excess proportion of total body fat. So how will you know you're obese? Usually you can find the best answer to this question by asking your doctor. Or by calculating your Body Mass Index (BMI), which is actually more important than just your weight. A person is considered obese when his or her BMI is equal to or greater than 30.

Calculate your BMI:

$$\textbf{BMI} = \frac{\textbf{weight in kilograms}}{\textbf{height in metres}^2}$$

Q. What actually is a calorie?

A: Calories are how energy is measured. The amount of calories in a food is the amount of energy that food contains for your body to use when you eat it. If you think of food as fuel, the energy content of the fuel is measured in calories.

Q. How much exercise should I do?

A: Studies show that even the most inactive people can gain significant health benefits if they accomodate just 30 minutes or more of physical activity per day. But that's just a minimum. Doing aerobic activity for most of the days and strength (anaerobic) training two to three days of the week is recommended for best results.

If you have been inactive for a while, you may want to start with less strenuous activities such as walking or swimming at a comfortable pace. Beginning at a slow pace will allow you to become physically fit without straining your body. Once you are in better shape, you can gradually do more strenuous activity.

Q. Why am I fat?

A: You, my dear, take in more calories than you burn unless it's hormone related.

Q. Does a diet soda have lesser calories?

A: Yes, it might not have the calories of regular soda but it has a thousand other things like caffeine, artificial sweeteners, sodium, and phosphoric acid, which are very harmful. Caffeine is a diuretic, so while you may be thinking that a diet soda quenches your thirst and helps keep you hydrated, the opposite happens. The next time you're feeling thirsty, switch that can of diet soda for a glass of water.

Q. Does building muscle reduce flexibility?
A: If you strength train without moving your joints through their full range of motion, you can indeed lose flexibility. However, strength training can improve flexibility if you move your joints properly. Stretch after a muscle-building workout to help keep yourself lithe.

PART II:

THE CCQ DIET

8

Week 1

Aim: Minor Modifications and Eating With the Sun

Target: Losing 1 to 2½ kilo

By now you should have gathered your tools, gone grocery shopping, and made sure that you have the foods you need. If you have to run out to the grocery store while you're hungry, you increase the chance of buying foods that are not diet friendly. Also, I hope you've invested in smaller-sized cutlery for yourself. You need to try eating smaller portions and you need to be visually satisfied.

> **Even if you can do, 10 percent of the diet in the first week you will see a big change in your body. Gradually work your way to 50 then 80 and finally 100 percent.**

Remember, this is an ideal diet and I understand that it is difficult to change your current lifestyle completely. So take it one step at a time. If you've been eating at 10 pm try to bring it down to 8 pm. Be gradual with change and it'll be easier for you to settle into the diet.

In the first week, I want you to work on one thing—eating on time. You should try to make this your priority factor. Once this is in place the rest of the diet will follow smoothly. I don't want to starve you or completely change your diet in the first week, because the body doesn't react well to drastic changes. Let's take it slowly and try first to get the timing right.

The first week will be your most trying one. It's these seven days that generally determine whether a person is going to be able to stay on it or throw in the towel. However, the first week is crucial to your success, and you need to follow it very closely. You might feel hungry, sometimes irritable because modification can deplete energy as you are cutting back on calories, your body's source of fuel. You will also be very easily tempted and will feel like giving it up almost every hour. Don't make drastic change. What I'm presenting here is an ideal eating plan. Take the model and taper down gradually.

But stick with it. It'll get better after the seventh day. This time, just commit for one week. After seven days, you'll start to see a difference. You'll also feel stronger and more energized and ready to see through the complete programme after the first week.

You need to be disciplined and concentrate on your goal. Plan your breakfast and meals the night before. Plan, plan, and plan some more. The trick lies in the planning or at least trying. You may falter but don't worry, you are only getting wiser and will succeed if your efforts are genuine.

Crucial Factors for Success in Week 1

1) **Visit your doctor**: Before starting the diet, please get a go ahead from your doctor. You should not have any serious ailments, low blood pressure, or be suffering from any other issues when you begin. This is a deficit calorie diet and you need to be careful not to push yourself if you are weak or ill. Only after getting a green light from your doctor should you begin.
2) **Weigh yourself every morning**: You've got to make a note of this every morning. Put it in your food diary. This is what you're starting at, and work from here towards your goal. Try and do it without fail.
3) **Maintain your food diary**: This is for accountability. Whatever you do, do not skip it,

and do not lie in it. Otherwise the whole process is a scam!

4) **Eat during the given time**: It's the only way you're going to make this happen.
5) **Carry water everywhere**: In order to lose weight without feeling sluggish, you need water. Without enough water in your body, it becomes increasingly difficult for your system to operate—leaving you tired and even light-headed.
6) **Buying new cutlery and pans**: You need a new pan because this is your no-oil diet. Not one drop. I want you to buy your own pan because when you're cooking for your family, you are going to be using oil for them. However, you are completely on a no-oil diet, and I don't want even one drop of it sneaking into your meals. By using your own pan, you can be completely sure that you remain oil-free.
7) **Tiffin with compartments**: If you work or go to college or are on the move, invest in a tiffin with two or three compartments. You will need to carry two types of cut fruit in it. You will be eating two cubes (ice cube size) of fruit starting from 9.30 am every half an hour between your major meals, which are breakfast, mid-morning snack, lunch, mid-afternoon snack and dinner. It has to be big enough to carry enough fruit in it.

8) **Go to bed early:** The trick is to sleep a little earlier than what your current time so that you don't get overly hungry after 4–6 hours after dinner.

THE FORMULA OF THE MEAL PLANS

As you go along you'll notice that all the meal plans follow a particular formula. They are a perfect combination of carbs, fibre, and protein. If you ever get lost along the way and want to remember what constitutes a balanced meal return to this box. Here I'll give you a simple formula to help you plan out your own meal.

Breakfast

Calcium + Carb + Protein
(Skimmed milk + multigrain bread or oats + egg white)

Mid-morning Snack

Negative calories
(green salad without dressing)

Lunch

Fibre based carbs + Protein + Calcium
(Wholegrain roti or rice + veggies + curd)

Mid-afternoon Snack

Nibbles!
(Green tea + multigrain crackers/roasted channa/ homemade dahi)

Dinner

Low carb, Low quantity, Low calories
(clear soup + steamed veggies or boiled chicken)

9) **Stock your larder**: Restock it with only whole grains and healthy food options because temptation is something very few of us can resist. Your family can do without crisps and bhujia for a week.

Now let's begin. Below are two examples of ideal meal plans. Try to follow it as best as you can. It'll help if you can stick to it and adapt it as you go along.

YOUR SPACE

Use this space to record your start weight

I weigh: ____________________

Date: ______________________

Week 1 Meal Plan 1

Time	Food
On rising: 7 and 7.30 am	Aloe vera juice (dilute half tsp of juice in half glass water) Or Green tea/regular tea (2 tsp skimmed milk, no sugar) + 3 almonds (soaked overnight) + ½ walnut

Time	Food
Breakfast between 8 and 8.30 am	100–150 ml milk + 30 ml oat bites Or 10–15 gm oats/dalia
9 am	2 cubes of fruit
9.30 am	2 cubes of fruit
10 am	2 cubes of fruit
10.30 am	2 cubes of fruit
11 am	Green salad (no dressing)
11.30 am	2 cubes of fruit
Lunch between 12 and 12.30 pm	1 (barley atta + oat barn) roti (equal proportions) + 1 bowl of veggies (no oil/no corn/no paneer/no potatoes) + ½ bowl of yoghurt/paneer made with low fat milk (made from skimmed milk)
1.30 pm	2 cubes of fruit
2 pm	2 cubes of fruit
2.30 pm	2 cubes of fruit
Snack between 3 and 3.30 pm	Green tea/regular tea (2 tsp skimmed milk, no sugar) + 2 oat biscuits
4 pm	2 cubes of fruit

Time	Food
4.30 pm	2 cubes of fruit
5 pm	2 cubes of fruit
5.30 pm	2 cubes of fruit
Dinner between 6.30 and 7 pm	200–250 ml of clear vegetable soup Or Green salad (no dressing with oil) + 2 slices of oatmeal bread + ½ chicken breast Or Sprouts

Meal Plan 2

Time	Food
On rising: 7 and 7.30 am	30 ml fresh wheat grass juice + ¼ tsp mix of flax, sunflower, and pumpkin seeds Or Green tea/regular tea (2 tsp skimmed milk, no sugar) + ¼ methi dana (soaked overnight)
Breakfast between 8 and 8.30 am	1 multigrain toast with veg/green chutney + 1 boiled egg white Or 100–150 ml milk

Time	Food
9 am	2 cubes of fruit
9.30 am	2 cubes of fruit
10 am	2 cubes of fruit
10.30 am	2 cubes of fruit
11 am	Green salad (no dressing)
11.30 am	2 cubes of fruit
Lunch between 12 and 12.30 pm	1 (ragi atta + oat flour + oat bran) roti (equal proportions) Or 1 cup brown rice + 1 bowl of mixed veggies (no oil/no corn/no paneer/no potatoes) + ½ bowl of yoghurt (made from skimmed milk)
1.30 pm	2 cubes of fruit
2 pm	2 cubes of fruit
2.30 pm	2 cubes of fruit
Snack between 3 and 3.30 pm	Green tea/regular tea (2 tsp skimmed milk, no sugar) + ½ cup murmura + roasted channas (mixed equally) Or 2 multigrain crackers
4 pm	2 cubes of fruit
4.30 pm	2 cubes of fruit

Time	Food
5 pm	2 cubes of fruit
5.30 pm	2 cubes of fruit
Dinner between 6.30 and 7 pm	200–250 ml of clear vegetable soup + Boiled chicken salad + 1 toast (optional) Or 250 ml paneer (made from skimmed milk) + Salad (no dressing) Or 1 bowl of steamed veggies

Day 4 in the first week is your big day. If you've been going according to plan, today is the day when you drop half a kilo. If you have a water retention problem then you'll drop water weight in the first couple of days. Only after that will you burn fat.

Day 7

You've made it till the end of the week. If you've followed the diet correctly and done your exercises, then today is the day when you're bound to drop 1 kg to 1½ kg. That is if you didn't cheat. Step on your scale and check it for yourself. If you have dropped weight then it is the best feeling to keep you going on to the next week. There is nothing like results to keep you going for another round of burn and to keep you motivated.

> **YOUR SPACE**
>
> **Use this space to record your weight at the end of Week 1**
>
> **I weigh:** ____________________
>
> **Date:** ______________________

After the first week, I hear yelps of joy and excitement from my clients who step on the weighing scale. They generally lose 2 or more if they have water retention issues. I know that they have been sincere and stuck to the routine. Some of the physical and mental changes that you'll notice about yourself after the first week are:

- weight drops by a kilo or more;
- you'll notice less flatulence in the mornings;
- you'll have more energy and strength; and
- you'll feel fresher in the mornings.

These are just some of the benefits you'll enjoy after the first week. As you keep going, your body will grow accustomed to the new dietary changes and the results will be manifold. So if you're ready, let's move on to Week 2.

If you can't...

- wake up early, then don't have a late breakfast. I'd rather you go straight into you eating fruit every 30 minutes. If you give too less a gap between breakfast and lunch then there will be a food group cluster, which I want you to avoid. But on week one I am flexible about your time. You can delay it by 30–45 minutes but remember breakfast is one of the most important meals of the day. Try to reach perfection gradually. You are doing great in the beginning. Minor modifications will work really well.

Week 1 Checklist

- ✔ I'm trying to eat my meals on time.
- ✔ I'm eating fruit every 20 to 30 minutes so as to never give my body a chance to get hungry.
- ✔ I'm drinking plenty of water, especially more in the first half of the day.
- ✔ I'm exercising.

9

Week 2

Aim: Tapering Down Your Dinner

Target: Losing 1½ kilos

By Week 2, you will be very successful and get your confidence levels up. Remember, this is an ideal diet, stick with it and you will gradually reach perfection. It's great that you're already on the road to losing weight, but if you sense your motivation beginning to slip—this eating plan will help you get back on track and leave you feeling inspired.

> **Remember, if you can do even 20 percent of the diet, you'll see a huge change in your body. Slowly work your way to 50 and then 100 percent.**

Week 2 is all about working on tapering your dinners down. I know that as much, or as hard as you might have tried, you probably slipped once during Week 1 in keeping to the time of your dinner. It's not your fault at all, and don't feel guilty about it. It's very rarely that you find people wrapping up dinner so early. Most people are still at work or driving home at that time. Also, most people don't associate 6 to 6.30 pm with dinner time. This is time when people like to binge on snacky foods like samosas and rolls. Office is winding down and people feel the need to take it a little easy on themselves. However, we are going to do things a little differently.

Eating an early dinner every day is one of the easiest ways to drop weight and lose inches on your waistline. Towards the latter part of the day, your body does not exert as much as it does during the earlier part, so fewer calories are burnt towards the evening. After your dinner, you are going to try to stop eating or eat a light meal. As I explained in Chapter 3 of this book, after sunset our bodies slow down their operations. During this time, the stomach is not ready to accept more food. It is in the process of assimilating and breaking down all the food it has received through the day and readying your body for the process of elimination the next morning. Anything eaten post sunset turns toxic and weighs heavily in your stomach. It is for that very reason that we have the old saying—**eat breakfast like a king, lunch like a prince, and dinner like**

a pauper. A golden rule for staying healthy. This is your ultimate target which will be reached gradually. A 10 p.m. dinner cannot become 6.30 p.m. one but in the beginning try to eat between 8–8.30 and then taper it down futher.

The benefits of eating early dinners are manifold. Here are a few of them:

- less flatulence in the morning as the food will be better digested;
- this will reduce the likelihood of gastro problems and acidity;
- sleep will be comfortable and uninterrupted, which does not happen when you eat right before bedtime;
- less lethargy because you went to bed early;
- no bloatedness; and
- face will not be puffy.

The Early Bird Catches the Worm

How many times have you started the day by jumping out of bed, late as usual, and rushing in to shower, getting ready, making breakfast, or not, getting stuck in traffic and getting in to work late? All this rush and chaos in the morning makes people stressed out, snappy, and it is just not a great start to the day. The direct result of eating an early dinner is that it sets about a cycle which is healthy. Think about it—if you have dinner at 6.30 pm, then ideally you should sleep by 10.30–11 pm, which would mean that you would eventually wake up earlier. And this would make it possible for you to work out and eat a good breakfast. Something that most people generally think is impossible to achieve. Sleeping early automatically makes you an early riser. And rising early is a great boon. If you can get into the habit you get quiet time to catch up on your work, read the papers, prepare and plan your day (and meals), gives you time to exercise, and kickstart your routine.

Crucial Factors for Success in Week 2:

1) **Eating a light and early dinner**: A light dinner is compatible with your body's inner system. Try it once to see the difference.
2) **Drinking enough water**: Keep yourself hydrated and fuelled with lots of water. Remember you're flushing of out toxins by drinking plenty of water.
3) **Exercising**: Losing weight is a combination of of both eating correctly and exercising. Don't ignore this vital component but at the same time don't do any overkill of a workout.
4) **Maintaining your food diary**: This is your progress record. Try to make this a habit for life.

5) **Weighing yourself every morning**: The best feeling you'll get is when you see the kilos drop. This is something you should look forward to everyday.

Note: The structure of your meal plan is almost the same, however, since we're going to be concentrating on the dinner, this is where you'll see the changes.

YOUR SPACE

Use this space to record your start weight

I weigh: ____________________________

Date: ________________________________

Week 2 Meal Plan 1

Time	Food
On rising: 7 and 7.30 am	30 ml fresh amla juice + 130 ml aloe vera juice (dilute half tsp of juice in half glass water) Or Green tea/regular tea (2 tsp skimmed milk, no sugar) + 1 fig + 2 almonds (soaked overnight)

Time	Food
Breakfast between 8 and 8.30 am	150 ml milk (skimmed milk) + 1 multigrain toast OR 30 gm oat bites + 150 ml milk Or 1 small bowl of oats + 150 ml milk
9 am	2 cubes of fruit
9.30 am	2 cubes of fruit
10 am	2 cubes of fruit
10.30 am	2 cubes of fruit
11 am	Green salad (no dressing)
11.30 am	2 cubes of fruit
Lunch between 12 and 12.30 pm	1 (barley atta + oat barn) roti (equal proportions) + 1 bowl of veggies (no oil/no corn/no paneer/no potatoes) + ½ bowl of yoghurt (made from skimmed milk)
1.30 pm	2 cubes of fruit
2 pm	2 cubes of fruit
2.30 pm	2 cubes of fruit

Time	Food
Snack between 3 and 3.30 pm	Green tea/regular tea (2 tsp skimmed milk, no sugar) Or 1 glass banana smoothie with 1 tbsp yoghurt
4 pm	2 cubes of fruit
4.30 pm	2 cubes of fruit
5 pm	2 cubes of fruit
5.30 pm	2 cubes of fruit
Dinner between 6.30 and 7 pm	200 ml clear vegetable soup Or Green salad (no dressing) + 2 slices of oatmeal bread Or Sprouts

Meal Plan 2

Time	Food
On rising: 7 and 7.30 am	Fresh wheat grass juice + 30 ml + ¼ tsp mix of flax, sunflower, and pumpkin seeds Or Green tea/regular tea (2 tsp skimmed milk, no sugar) + ¼ methi dana (soaked overnight)

Time	Food
Breakfast between 8 and 8.30 am	1 multigrain toast + 1 boiled egg white Or 100–150 ml milk + 1 one small bowl of oats
9 am	2 cubes of fruit
9.30 am	2 cubes of fruit
10 am	2 cubes of fruit
10.30 am	2 cubes of fruit
11 am	Green salad (no dressing)
11.30 am	2 cubes of fruit
Lunch between 12 to 12.30 pm	1 (ragi atta + oat flour + oat bran) roti (equal proportions) + 1 bowl of veggies (no oil/no corn/no paneer/no potatoes) + ½ bowl of yoghurt (made from skimmed milk)
1.30 pm	2 cubes of fruit
2 pm	2 cubes of fruit
2.30 pm	2 cubes of fruit
Snack between 3 and 3.30 pm	Green tea/regular tea (2 tsp skimmed milk, no sugar) + vegetable oil free patty Or 2 multigrain crackers

Time	Food
4 pm	2 cubes of fruit
4.30 pm	2 cubes of fruit
5 pm	2 cubes of fruit
5.30 pm	2 cubes of fruit
Dinner between 6.30 and 7 pm	200 ml clear vegetable soup Or 60 gm steamed white fish Or 250 ml paneer (made from skimmed milk) + 1 bowl of steamed veggies Cut the carbs at dinner time and emphasise on perfection with time for dinner and not eating after that.

Day 4 is here again! Your big day. If you've been going according to plan, today is the day when you drop another kilo. Remember, you also have an extra accumulated deficit of 500 calories from your previous week. This will maximize the calorie burn and speed up the process of losing weight. So what are you waiting for? Get on to that scale and weigh yourself.

Day of Deviation

So you've made it to the last day of Week 2. Congratulations! By now, if you've followed the plan, you should have lost another 2–2½ kg. I have to remind you once again that if you haven't, you need to go back to Week 1 and start all over again as you're not doing something right.

Because you've been diligent and sincere (I hope you have), today is the day when you can treat yourself to whatever you want. I call it your Day of Deviation. Sounds like fun, doesn't it? However, this doesn't mean that you go out and eat a family-sized pizza or a bucket of chicken. On the Day of Deviation, I let my clients indulge in whatever they want…in controlled portions.

The Importance of the Day of Deviation

I have a client who came to me worried. He said, 'Nishi, I'm going on a two-week holiday. There's no way I can fight the temptation of all the exotic food that's going to be around me. I've lost so much weight and now it's just going to come back again. Such a waste of effort.'

I told him that there was no reason for him to be disheartened. He was going to be on holiday so it would be a shame if he didn't indulge himself. I told him, 'Eat whatever you want but *only during breakfast and lunch* and, of course, in controlled portions.' For breakfast, I told him to eat a good portion of fruit and then dig into bacon, cold cuts or cheese, muffins, etc. For lunch, he should first have a good portion of salad or soup before the main meal.

He called me excitedly when he got back. 'I haven't gained a kilo! And I ate everything I wanted to. What did I do right?'

When I told him the answer he laughed. Because it was so simple.

It's because he was eating the most at a time when his body burned the most calories. So in effect, he wasn't gaining any extra calories!

It's important that you understand that despite the name (Day of Deviation), you shouldn't spend an entire day once a week eating whatever you please. When you plan a day of deviation in your diet once in one week, you can look forward to rewarding yourself for your hard work. Every time you feel the temptation throughout the week to stray from your diet, you'll be able to remind yourself that you will have that treat on your cheat day and you'll find the temptation less strong than if you're told you can never touch food that you like to eat again. Also apetite shrinks with time and a person becomes quite conscious of healthy and unhealthy foods.

If you don't have any deviation day to look forward to, you can be in danger of binge eating. You could find yourself reaching for 'just one' unhealthy snack and end up spending days over eating unhealthy food that will ruin your diet. After you're done binging, you'll feel guilty and you may attempt unhealthy behaviours, such as starving yourself or crash dieting, both of which can be harmful to your health and fitness plan. I believe in eating and eating right. Rewarding yourself and not being too hard on yourself can help give you the focus and determination you need to succeed during the rest of the week.

Another reason why I feel it is a good idea to have a diet deviation day is because it can teach you how to have self control when it comes to eating unhealthy foods.

Learning how to portion control your meals, meal planning, eating in moderation, and monitoring your weight are all part of self control that's crucial to losing weight for long term results, plus weight maintenance.

Also, why I say you should have a diet deviation day is because you are only human, right? And a little bit of deviation can never hurt anyone.

The Fine Print

Say you've been craving for seafood pasta, a slice of chocolate cake, and wine—you can have it all. Now here's the fine print—**you can eat all of the above but in measured quantities and only for lunch.** So what you should do is get a quarter plate of pasta (try to opt for red or no sauce because ut's a healthier option), a thin slice of cake, and a glass of wine or whatever else you fancy. That way you've had everything you've craved for but haven't thrown your diet out of the window because you have had a salad or a soup prior to your indulgence. By doing so you are eating for taste and not for filling up your stomach. This is also a way to teach you how to eat in restaurants when you're off the diet. It teaches you that you can actually eat anything you want but in the right quantities. This way you'll never crave the extra food and never put on extra weight.

Now the reason why you can treat yourself at lunch is because your BMR is at its peak. So whatever you eat, you are also burning it off with the maximum potential. Treating yourself at night will mean that your body takes more effort to burn these extra calories.

In the Day 7 meal plan you'll find that I have nothing to offer you in the lunch section. This is your space and you can eat whatever you want. So go ahead and indulge yourself but with a strict eye on the portions.

Meal Plan 3

Time	Food
On rising: 7 and 7.30 am	Fresh wheat grass juice + 30 ml + ¼ tsp mix of flax, sunflower and pumpkin seeds Or Green tea/regular tea (2 tsp skimmed milk, no sugar) + ¼ methi dana (soaked overnight)
Breakfast between 8 and 8.30 am	1 multigrain toast + 1 boiled egg white Or 150 ml milk + 1 multigrain toast
9 am	2 cubes of fruit
9.30 am	2 cubes of fruit
10 am	2 cubes of fruit
10.30 am	2 cubes of fruit
11 am	Green salad (no dressing)
11.30 am	2 cubes of fruit
Lunch between 12 and 12.30 pm	Your treat (IN CONTROLLED PORTIONS)
1.30 pm	2 cubes of fruit
2 pm	2 cubes of fruit
2.30 pm	2 cubes of fruit

Time	Food
Snack between 3 and 3.30 pm	Green tea/regular tea (2 tsp skimmed milk, no sugar) + ½ cup murmura + roasted channa (mixed equally)
4 pm	2 cubes of fruit
4.30 pm	2 cubes of fruit
5 pm	2 cubes of fruit
5.30 pm	2 cubes of fruit
Dinner between 6 and 6.30 pm	200 ml clear chicken soup (no chicken stock) + 1 bowl of steamed veggies Or 250 gm paneer (made from skimmed milk) + 1 bowl of steamed veggies Or if you are not feeling hungry since you ate out you can just have a cup of skinned milk and fruit.

YOUR SPACE

Use this space to record your weight at the end of Week 2

I weigh: ______________________________

Date: ________________________________

Changes in Your Body After Week 2

Some of the physical and mental changes that you'll notice about yourself after Week 2 are:

- weight drops by 2 kg or more;
- your skin has a nice glow to it;
- your shirts will no longer hug your stomach like they used to;
- you'll notice less flatulence in the mornings;
- you'll have more energy and strength;
- you'll feel fresher in the mornings; and
- a constant feeling of being light and boundy.

IF YOU CAN'T...

- not eat anything after your early dinner, grab a fruit or drink a glass of skimmed milk later. But don't have any complex carbs so late, anything uncooked or any nuts. It'll spoil the momentum you've set.

WEEK 2 CHECKLIST

- ✔ I'm wrapping up dinner early.
- ✔ And in turn waking up earlier to accommodate breakfast.
- ✔ Day of Deviation...I've eaten whatever I craved for during the past two weeks after checking with my counsellor. Bliss!
- ✔ I've been exercising and I feel fitter already.
- ✔ And I'm drinking plenty of water, especially more in the first half of the day.

10

A One-Day Detox

Well done! You've completed two successful weeks of the diet. By the estimation you should have lost 3–4 kg by now. You should, by now, also be familiar with the structure of the diet and how the foods are placed through the day and what kind of foods you should be eating. Before we get on with Week 3, you need to do a short detox immediately after your deviation day. I recommend this to everyone who has successfully finished two weeks of the diet.

Why Detox?

Ever wonder why we have so many fasts in India?

If you think about it, almost all religions in the world include fasting for spiritual, physical, and mental recovery. In India, we have a number of days on which we fast—Navratras, Janmashtami, Karvachauth and Shivratri are a few examples. In short, detox means cleansing the body. But it should not be done more than once or twice a week. Detoxing is important for the body and has been a practice from time immemorial. The age-old idea of fasting, I believe, has more to do with purification of the system than spiritual reasons.

Ayurveda also encourages fasting to removes toxins and poisons that accumulate in the body for a period of time. One of the toxins it describes is 'ama'. Today, our food is mainly non-organic, processed, with chemical additives, grown with pesticides and chemical fertilizers and these are particularly harmful and cause major lifestyle diseases. Chemicals introduce toxins into your body, slowing down the core functions. Undigested and partially digested food lingers in the body, leading to the formation of ama. Ayurveda views ama as one of the most threatening opponents to good health, linking the majority of health disorders in some way to the presence of this substance.

Think of ama as a by-product of modern day evils.

How do you know if your body is being burdened with excess ama? Take this short quiz to find out.

Q1. Do you wake up feeling tired in the mornings?
- a) Yes
- b) No

Q2. Does it take you a while to get up from bed? Do you generally need tea to wake you up?
- a) Yes
- b) No

Q3. Is your tongue coated when you wake up in the morning?
- a) Yes
- b) No

Q4. Do you often feel lethargic and unmotivated, especially after a meal?
- a) Yes
- b) No

Q5. How many times a year do you catch a cold?
- a) More than thrice
- b) Once or twice

Q6. Do you frequently suffer from constipation?
- a) Yes
- b) No

Q7. Do you tend to feel weak or listless for no apparent reason?

a) Yes
b) No

Q8. Do you sometimes get a mild black out, which disappears quickly, when getting up from a resting position?
a) Yes
b) No

Q9. Do you frequently feel sad or weary?
a) Yes
b) No

Q10. Do you exercise regularly?
a) No
b) Yes

If you've answered mainly **a**s, then you're a victim of ama. But don't let this get you down. In fact, most people today suffer from it. And it's only inevitable because of the rushed and harried lives we lead. However, ama too can be controlled, and you can do it by changing your eating patterns to eating on time and eating right.

The other way to combat ama is calorie restriction. Restriction of food is one of the oldest methods recommended by physicians as an integral part of the treatment and prevention of disease. And hence the concept of fasting.

The principle of a detox diet is simple. A detox diet involves calorie restriction, which is the most effective way of getting rid of toxins and gives the system a break from work associated with digestion. This clears the skin, increases our energy levels, improves brain function, and makes us more alert. The body and mind during a detox are in a transformational state as physical and emotional toxins are being released from the body.

A detox diet involves cleansing the system of impurities and giving it the foods that take the minimum effort for your body to digest like raw fruits and veg (nothing cooked).

The idea of a good detox diet is to eat pure and natural foods that will aid the function of the kidneys and liver. The main aim is to put as less strain on your digestive system as possible. However, nowadays most of the detox plans that are floating around involve being on a liquid diet the whole day. This is not healthy. I don't encourage too many days of detoxing either. You need your energy and can't live on an empty stomach.

NOTE

A detox shouldn't be done too often as it slows down the metabolic rate. It can be done once in every week.

After Week 2 of the diet, I generally put my clients on a half detox. It should be done on a fixed day once a week. Not more. Think of it as a day of compensation for your body, after your Sunday treat.

In this detox plan, I intend not to shock your body into starvation mode but to keep it simple. It's almost the same as your diet however with one tiny difference. You will eat both breakfast and lunch, and will continue eating fruit every 20 to 30 minutes. After which you will taper it down. The only meal that you don't have is dinner. This is so that your body doesn't crave for food and makes the process gradual. Remember, this is only for one day. After which you will go back to the diet.

Drinking water during a detox is crucial. It is no secret that drinking 2 to 3 litres of water a day can dramatically improve your health, and the signs will be obvious: glowing complexion and clear skin, better immunity, better digestion, less aches and pains, weight loss, less cellulite, better concentration, and renewed vitality and energy. And on a detox, it's even better.

You should try and drink as much water, or more, as possible through the duration of the detox. This will speed up the process of flushing out toxins.

The One-Day Half Detox Plan

(Avoid tea, snacks and dinner)

Monday	Time	Food
	On rising: 7 and 7.30 am	Amla juice + 2 almonds + ½ walnut + 1 fig (soaked overnight)
	Breakfast between 8 to 8.30 am	150 ml milk (skimmed) + 1 multigrain toast + Small bowl of oats
	9 am	2 cubes of fruit
	9.30 am	2 cubes of fruit
	10 am	2 cubes of fruit
	10.30 am	2 cubes of fruit
	11 am	Green salad (no dressing)
	11.30 am	2 cubes of fruit
	Lunch between 12 and 12.30 pm	1 (ragi atta + oat flour + oat bran) roti (equal proportions) + 1 bowl of veggies (no oil/no corn/no paneer/no potatoes) + ½ bowl of yoghurt (made from skimmed milk)

Monday	Time	Food
	1 pm	2 cubes of fruit
	1.30 pm	2 cubes of fruit
	2 pm	2 cubes of fruit
	2.30 pm	2 cubes of fruit
	3 pm	2 cubes of fruit
	3.30 pm	2 cubes of fruit
	4 pm	2 cubes of fruit
	4.30	2 cubes of fruit
	5 pm	2 cubes of fruit
	5.30 pm	2 cubes of fruit
	6 pm	2 cubes of fruit
	6.30 pm	2 cubes of fruit

SOS

If you are very hungry in the first detox. You can have a glass of milk at 6.30–7 p.m.

11

Week 3

Aim: Working on Portions

Target: Losing 1½ kilos

A high five to you for getting to Week 3! By now, you must have understood the format of eating correctly and what you should be eating and most importantly…when.

> **Try to do at least 50 percent of the diet. The results you'll see will push you on to aim for 100 percent.**

Today, everything is supersize. There's an add on to everything. Add fries for only Rs 30 or go for the combo (with coke, fries, and a few chicken wings thrown in) and you get Rs 80 off from your total. Why wouldn't people opt for something with a discount? Nutritionist and author of the book *The Portion Teller* Dr Lisa Young says in an article in the *Huffington Post*: 'Our plates have increased. So have our mugs, glasses, and wine goblets. Our cabinets and dishwashers are now larger to accommodate our satellite-sized dishes. And car seats for our kids, who are now pudgier than ever, have also increased. And even caskets have become super-sized! Many of us don't understand what a healthy portion size is, and for good reason. A pasta portion in a restaurant is easily three cups, and many steaks are at least a pound. That is much too much food. The problem is that we've gotten used to these jumbo portion sizes and we think that a "portion" is whatever is put in front of us. I tracked the history of food portions increasing since the 20th century and found that portions are much, much bigger than they were in the past—2–5 times bigger, to be exact. And so are people! No surprise.'

Portion control is all about being visually satisfied. In a way, you're tricking your mind. If your mind thinks it has enough food it won't think it's being starved, and won't send out craving signals. But if it thinks you're starving the body, it'll immediately want more. This is again a symptom of the ancient fight or flight syndrome. After all, our first priority is to survive, and so our body will work towards that goal.

With a little practice, portion control is easy to do and can help you be successful in reaching and then maintaining a proper weight. I have already told you earlier how you can control your portions. Here is the full list:

1) **Snacking:** Control your portions in a meal by making an effort to snack frequently on healthy, low calorie foods. This way you will be able to control your appetite and eat small amount of food at one meal.

2) **Minus one**: Whatever you eat every day, take one from it. If you eat three spoonfuls of rice, make it two. If you generally have five rotis for lunch, let one go. It's as simple as that but this small step is significant because you're making a cut, and training your mind to recognize the fact that one less of everything cannot harm you; you won't die of hunger minus one.

3) **Divide your plate in half**: And fill one side with fruits or vegetables, leaving the rest for equal parts for protein and carbs. This will show you what a properly balanced meal looks like and will give you a better understanding of what you're actually eating.

4) **Smaller plates and bowls**: This is my time-tested trick. Smaller plates means less food. A small cup of vegetable full to the brim gives you more visual satisfaction than a half full big cup. We call it visual satisfaction. A research conducted by a team of health experts rounded up a group of people (ages 21 to 35) and gave them all various sizes of bowls and asked them to help themselves of a variety of ice cream. What it showed was that at the end, the people with bigger bowls served themselves 31 percent more ice cream than the ones with smaller bowls.

5) **Don't multi task**: When you're watching TV you're not concentrating on your food and consequently are not paying attention to the amount of food that you're consuming.

6) **Small but many meals**: My rule about eating a few pieces of fruit every 20 mintues makes sure that it keeps your blood sugar even throughout the day. It keeps your energy up and doesn't make you ravenous. People who eat a few small meals a day are much more likely to maintain portion control because they never become too hungry.

7) **Learn your sizes**: Invest in measuring scales such as a measuring cup or a weighing scale for food.

It helps to keep a track of things. With use, you'll slowly get the hang of estimates without their help. Keep an eye out for how much constitutes a tablespoon or teaspoon.

8) **Pouring oil**: Never pour oil directly out of the bottle. You can never keep track of how much you're going to use if you do that. When using oil, always use teaspoons or tablespoons.

9) **The right salad**: Research has shown that people who start lunch with a low calorie salad consume 7 percent fewer calories during their meal. Eat your salad 30 minutes before your main meal and you'll never end up binging. Avoid high-calorie salads with extras like bacon, cheese, mayo, and dressings.

These tips can help to regulate your portions.

SIZE QUIZ

One slice of bread should be about as big as:

1. Notebook
2. Your palm
3. A BlackBerry
4. An index card

The correct answer is 4.

Remember, portion-control is less to do with eating less than eating intelligently.

The diet that you need to follow from Week 3 onwards should follow the same principles of eating on time, eating the right grains, and in the correct portions. If you can follow this, you will lose the rest of your weight in no time. But don't let my foods limit you. I have just set the format for healthy eating and how you can lose weight effectively. You already know what you should eat and what you shouldn't (use my charts as guides). So keeping those parameters in mind, feel free to experiment—change your vegetables and grains to make your food exciting and flavourful.

Ideally, I suggest you follow this format of planning your meals for four weeks. If you've lost the desired amount of weight or reached your ideal weight then you can move on to gradually increasing your portion sizes and reintroducing visible fats into your diet. A word of caution, you have to be extra careful about this step as this is where most people falter. Maintaining your ideal weight is tougher than losing weight. I shall discuss this at length in Part III. I once counselled a 65-year-old German lady, who was also a swami. She lost 15–16 kg in 4 months. She was so happy with the results that she wanted to do more. It took me 2 hours to convince her to add oil and to bring in some flexibility in her meals.

Crucial Factors for Success in Week 3:

1. *Portion control*
2. *Drinking enough water*
3. *Exercising*
4. *Maintaining your food diary*
5. *Weighing yourself every morning*

YOUR SPACE

Use this space to record your weight at the end of Week 3

I weigh: ______________________________

Date: ________________________________

Now that you've finished three successful weeks of the diet, you must be familiar with the routine. Remember, **after every day of deviation, you should follow it up with a day of compensation**. This is to ensure that you shed the extra calories that you've consumed during your deviation meal, and to start the process of eating healthy again.

Changes in your body after Week 3

Some of the physical and mental changes that you'll notice about yourself after Week 2 are:

- Weight drops by a kilo or more;
- Your skin glows even more;
- Your hair has a nice shine to it;
- You have more concentration power;
- More energy to pack in more things in one day;
- Nails feel less brittle;
- Tongue no longer has a white coat in the mornings; and
- A positive change in attitude and confidence.

IF YOU CAN'T...

- Figure out your meal plans, go back to Week 1 and look at the formula.

WEEK 3 CHECKLIST

- ✔ I'm working on my portions...
- ✔ ...and my food choices.
- ✔ My tongue is clear in the mornings!
- ✔ I have my dinner before going out in the evenings.
- ✔ Exercising.
- ✔ Becoming better time and food for dinner.

12

A One-Hour Exercise Routine

Exercise is my first love. I got into it when I was barely a teenager. I had an obsessive quest to find the most effective way to exercise and tried everything under the sun from cycling, running, doing yoga till I found the one thing that truly made me happy—aerobics. I haven't stopped doing it since. I feel that people don't like to exercise because they consider it a task. They go to gyms and plod on treadmills, and look dull as death while doing it. That I feel will never work in making exercise a part of your life. The trick is to think of working out as a fun activity, which will immediately entail that you take up an exercise you enjoy doing. After all, you'll have an easier time sticking to your exercise plan and beating boredom if you're having fun while doing it. But 'moderate intensity physical activity' can also include brisk walking and anything else that gets your heart rate up to an aerobic level.

Besides consuming a low-calorie, low-carb diet and being mindful about eating on time, you must exercise. You don't have to train for the marathon; half an hour of brisk walking (not strolling) every day is all you need to burn calories, build muscle, control cravings, and increase endorphin levels. It is one of the most basic elements of living a healthy life. To live a truly healthy life, you need to be familiar with the basics of good exercise, as well as how regular exercise can benefit your body. Proper exercise is unfortunately one of the most ignored factors of a healthy lifestyle, which is one of the main reasons why obesity is becoming such a common problem.

I suggest taking one hour out of your schedule to work out. Ideally, I would suggest you go out of your comfort zone (your house)—to the park for a walk or work with a trainer—however, if you feel more comfortable at home this is what you have to do. As you get used to exercising, gradually increase the intensity of the workout. I'm going to divide this one hour into three parts:

1. 15 minutes of warm up
2. 30 minutes of cardio
3. 15 minutes of stretching and cooling down

Let's take it one by one now.

1. Warming Up

Warming up goes a long way toward preparing the body for exercising, both physically and mentally. It also helps prevent injuries. To prepare for exercise and get the most out of your fitness training it is important to warm up, cool down, and stretch properly. Besides preventing injuries, correct exercise preparation will help you get the best out of your body's workout.

Warming up raises the heart rate, gets blood flowing to the working muscles, and prepares the body for exercise. It should be for a minimum of five minutes and replicate the movements or activities of the main session. When you warm up, you are literally warming up the temperature of both your body and your muscles.

Often a warm up activity is simply the activity you are about to do but at a slower pace. For example, if you're about to go for a brisk run, warm up with a light jog, and if you're going to go for a swim, do a couple of slow freestyle warm up laps.

I insist on a warm up. It should be done slowly and in a relaxed state so as to not injure any muscles. Here's a warm up routine that you can do anywhere. Try and make it a part of your life.

Step 1

- Stand with your feet slightly apart. Shoulders relaxed. Chest out. Stomach tucked in. Breathe normally.
- Stretch your arms in front of you, lock your fingers and stretch upwards as much as you can. Stand on your toes and try and keep going higher. Do this without any jerks. Hold the pose till you can and release.
- Come back to the first position then slowly and try to touch the floor (keeping your spine as straight as possible). If you can't do it (see picture), it's okay. You can gradually work your way to the floor. Hold the pose till you can and release.

Step 2

- Stand with your feet slightly apart. Shoulders relaxed. Stomach tucked in. Breathe normally. Then place your hands firmly on your waist and arch your back as much as you can and drop your head. Hold the pose till you can and release.
- Come back to the standing position. Lock your fingers in front of you and keeping your back straight bend forwards. Hold the pose till you can and release.

Step 3

- Stand with your feet wide apart. Shoulders relaxed. Stomach tucked in. Breathe normally. Turn your right foot out and bend towards the right knee. Keep your back straight and look towards the direction of your right foot. Hold the pose till you can and release.
- Now, turn your left foot out and bend the left knee. Keep your back straight and look straight ahead. Hold the pose till you can and release.

Step 4

- Stand with your feet together. Shoulders relaxed. Stomach tucked in. Breathe normally. Bend your right knee and grab your ankle. Hold the pose till you can and release.
- Now, repeat the same movement with your left knee. Hold the pose till you can and release.

Step 5

- Now, do the reverse. Stand with your feet together. Shoulders relaxed. Stomach tucked in. Breathe normally. Hold your right knee with both your hands and pull it back to your stomach or as much as you can. Hold the pose till you can and release.
- Repeat the same movement with your left knee. Hold the pose till you can and release.

Step 6

- Stand with your feet together. Shoulders relaxed. Stomach tucked in. Breathe normally.
- Cross your left foot over your right, keeping your back straight and bend over. If you can, grab the back of your calf muscles. You should feel a mild stretch in your hamstring muscles. Hold the pose till you can and release. Come back to standing position.
- Now, cross your right foot over your left one and hold the pose till you can and release.

Step 7

- Stand with your feet wide apart. Shoulders relaxed. Stomach tucked in. Breathe normally. Stretch your arms out on both sides.
- Slowly bend to your right using your right arm to guide you. Do not put any pressure on it. Keep your left arm straight and aligned over your left ear. Look straight. Hold the pose till you can and gently come back.
- Now, do the same with your left side.

Step 8

- Stand with your feet wide apart. Shoulders relaxed. Stomach tucked in. Breathe normally. Stretch your arms out on both sides.
- Keeping your arms stretched out, bend to your right. Do not bend your knee. Keep looking ahead of you. Hold the pose till you can and gently come back up.
- Now, do the same on your left side.

Step 9

- Find a stable surface like a chair or a table. Stand with your feet together. Breathe normally. Bend from your waist above, keeping your back straight, for a half push up. Repeat 10 times.

Step 10

- Stand with your feet together. Shoulders relaxed. Stomach tucked in. Breathe normally. Gently rotate your head in clockwise motion. Do this 3 times then go anti-clockwise.

Step 11

- Stand with your feet together. Shoulders relaxed. Stomach tucked in. Breathe normally. Gently rotate your ankles and wrists in clockwise motion. Do this 3 times then go anti-clockwise.

2. Cardio

Exercise for me is a challenge. When I'm out, brisk walking in the park, my aim is to keep up with the person who is jogging in front of me. It can get very difficult but I keep at it. It's my challenge! You too need a challenge while working out. Exercising at a comfortable pace doesn't help you lose weight. You need to get out of your comfort zone to make that happen. From running and walking, swimming, elliptical cross-training, biking—to name a few—the physical benefits of cardio exercise are a plenty.

Extra weight is a contributing factor to conditions such as heart disease, high blood pressure, stroke, diabetes, and some forms of cancer. As you lose weight, your risk of developing these diseases decreases. In addition, weight-bearing aerobic exercise, such as walking, can reduce your risk of osteoporosis and its complications. Low-impact aerobic exercises, such as swimming, cycling, and pool exercises can help keep you fit if you have arthritis, without putting excessive stress on your joints.

Regular aerobic exercise causes your lungs to process more oxygen with less effort, your heart to pump more blood with fewer beats, and the blood supply directed to your muscles to increase. As a result, by performing cardiovascular exercises, you are increasing your body's endurance and efficiency. Apart from keeping you fit and making you lose weight here are a few benefits for indulging in cardio activity:

- reduced risk of heart disease;
- improved blood cholesterol levels;
- improved heart function;
- reduced risk of osteoporosis;
- improved muscle mass;
- higher BMR; and
- stronger bone structure.

Basically, you need a minimum of 30 minutes of controlled cardio activity to keep you fit. Here I give you a routine and guaranteed way of burning the most amount of calories in 30 minutes.

Step 1: Get on to the treadmill and work it up to the speed where you're almost running. Try to maintain this speed. Remember, never run on the treadmill.

Step 2: Brisk walk at that speed for 20 minutes.

Step 3: It's only after 20 minutes of being at that speed will the process of burning calories begins. So you need to keep it up for more than 30 minutes to burn fat. If you can, push the speed up a bit more for a minute and bring it down. Do this consistently for 10 minutes. If you can't walk any faster, then stay at the same pace and keep it up for the next 5 minutes and gradually bring it down.

Note: If you don't have a treadmill, follow the same pattern on a brisk walk.

3. Stretching

Whether you are new to working out or have been playing a sport your entire life, adding a good before-and-after routine to your workout will give you the best chance of avoiding injuries and may even help improve your performance. Stretching is vital after your heavy work out. This should be only after working out. You should try to avoid stretching cold muscles because they can get pulled and torn.

Stretching properly will reduce muscle injuries and provide the benefits of an increase in flexibility, correct exercise posture, and relaxed muscles. However, stretching has to be done correctly otherwise this too can be harmful to your body. Here are some tips on stretching properly:

1) **Stop if it hurts**. Stretching should never hurt. If you have reached a point in your stretch where it hurts, relax to where it feels comfortable and hold the stretch.

2) **Hold it**. Maintain each stretch for 10–30 seconds, till you can. Holding a stretch for less than that won't sufficiently lengthen the muscle. Stretch the muscles gradually and don't force it. Avoid bobbing or bouncing while stretching. This may damage the muscle you are stretching.

3) **Remember to breathe**. Breathing is a necessary part of any workout, including stretching.

4) **Practice equality**. You should not neglect any side of your body. Make sure you stretch both sides equally, so that all your muscles are evenly ready for action.

Cooling Down

In Yoga, the shavasana is practiced after every major asan. This is to ensure that the heartbeat comes back to its normal pace and that the muscles relax. Yoga, in fact, had hit the nail right on the head with the concept of cooling down.

In all my years of teaching aerobics, I have seen many cases where absolutely fit people injure themselves after a session of work out. This generally happens because they never cooled down their systems properly. Think of your body as if it were a car. If you keep it running in the heat for too long it'll overheat and malfunction. The same is the case with your body. You need to give it the time to cool down after hard work.

You need to slow down your body after a work out or exercise: 5–10 minutes of slowed-down, easy activities will go a long way in helping your body recover from a work out. Your cooling down routine can vary from work out to work out. It should include light aerobic activity and stretching. If you're running at a quick pace, you can slow down to a steady walk to cool down. Cooling down and stretching at the end of a workout help to slow your heart rate to a normal speed, return your breathing to its regular pace, avoid stiffness and soreness of the muscles, reduce any risk of dizziness and lightheadedness, and relax the muscles.

WHAT IS THE BEST TIME TO WORK OUT?

The best time to work out is generally the time that works for you. Because this is what will actually get you to exercise! I prefer mornings and early evenings. But you need to pick a time and stick to it. Consistency is key.

Take a moment to think about the time during the day when you're at your most productive and feeling energetic. If you're not a morning person, you know best that you're never going to get out of bed a little earlier to exercise. I don't even need to tell you that. Also, you need to allot an hour when you aren't bogged down by responsibilities. You can't be answering emails on the treadmill!

PART III

MAINTAINING YOUR WEIGHT

13

How to Maintain Your Weight?

Yo-Yoing

Radhika, 35 years old, is back in my clinic for the third time for a counseling session. This time she's here to lose 10 kg (which she had previously lost in her second session with me but has gained back in the course of the year). She's dedicated, follows my diet to the T, and yet she's always back after a year or two with all the lost weight (and more) back on.

This is one of the most common scenarios I have to deal with. In my counseling sessions, I always have one client who has been on a programme with me before. And it includes clients who have successfully lost their excess weight.

Okay, you've reached your weight loss goal. Now all you have to do is make sure you're one of the 5-10 percent of 'weight-losers' who manage to keep the extra weight off. Maintaining their ideal weight is where almost everyone falters. While losing weight does take focus and dedication, it's important to remember that losing weight isn't really a start-and-end process. Sure, you have a weight-loss goal to reach, but once you get there, you don't just stop eating right and working out.

I have an almost hundred percent success rate when making clients lose weight. It's because I'm vigilant, chase them on their progress, and maintain a strict watch on what's going into their mouths. When they're with me, I know they'll lose weight and be healthy. The trouble begins when they finish the programme and I am not there to hold their hands or tell them to think again when they eat high calorie food consistently. It begins with them putting on 1 or 2 kg. And that never worries them. If you lose 15 kg and then gain 3, it's easy to think that's no big deal. But it's a slippery slope. That should be the first warning sign. What you should actually tell yourself is 'look I lost 15 kg to get to my ideal weight, and gaining 3 is not okay'.

This is the vicious cycle of losing weight. And it usually happens because of the reason that people lose weight in the first place. Most people I know go on a diet because of a short-term reason. They either go on a diet because there's a wedding, a holiday, or they are just trying to be thinner than their competition.

Very few people come to my programme with a long-term goal, with the view of being healthy. Ninety percent of the people I've counselled want to lose their weight quickly but don't imbibe my philosophy of making healthy eating a lifestyle, an ethic I reiterate all the time.

Some people start regaining weight simply because they start eating a little bit more and exercising a little less, often without even noticing it. That's the reason I ask people to do the weight loss plan with the mind and not with just the mouth and for quick results.

Remember, everyone can lose weight—any amount of it—but the tough part or trick is to keep it at your ideal number. Many people manage to get where you are now, very few manage to maintain that success, and much less keep moving ahead. What will determine your success is how well you identify the particular challenges you face and find effective ways to manage them. The upside is that you already have the tools and information you're going to need to maintain your success.

I live and breathe my programme, and my weight generally never fluctuates. That's because I aim to stay healthy for the long haul.

You have to reconsider the whole notion of dieting as a temporary fix. Think of what you're doing as a permanent lifestyle shift because that is the only thing that is going to keep you thin for life. You'll have to be extra vigilant. A diet is successful when you can maintain your weight for life. Otherwise, sure enough, you'll give up and try another one, and fall into the trap of dieting for life.

Post Diet Changes

After weeks, or months, of controlling your calorie intake, knowing what to do when you hit your dream target can be scary but you can't stick with your dieting calorie amount forever.

While some people prefer to immediately increase their calorie intake, others prefer to do it in steps. In many ways, taking it gradually is a good idea as it helps you to concentrate on getting your extra calories by slowly increasing the portion sizes of the foods you're already eating rather than suddenly going beserk.You have to shift the focus from weight loss to weight maintenance. But first, you need to bring back a few elements that you cut out from your diet or did differently.

1) **Decrease the amount of water** recommended in the main diet. You don't need so much now that you're at your ideal weight.
2) **Reintroduce fat:** Fat is essential to your development and you cannot leave it out of your

diet completely. It gives your hair and face the needed shine. Get back to buttering your toast once a week, and not more.

3) **Reintroduce pulses:** Pulses, again, are essential for a balanced diet, and should be consumed again after the diet.
4) **Reintroduce beans:** Bring back your channa, lobia, and rajma—the heavy beans—but only during lunch time as they are more difficult to digest.
5) **Push up the exercise tempo:** According to research, the most important factor in maintaining weight is a consistently high level of regular activity and exercise. The only way you can keep to your weight stable is by burning more calories by exercising more.

Increasing the Food Quantity Gradually

All the time you've been dieting, your body has become more and more efficient at using the limited number of calories you've been supplying and it becomes accustomed to meeting its energy needs by burning fat. Remember how difficult it was to get the body to start burning fat at the start of the diet—those awful first few days? Similarly, at the end of your diet it takes a while to shift from burning fat to meeting all your calorie needs from food again. By the end of your diet, you'll have a very accurate idea of your daily calorie shortfall. Eventually, you'll want to increase your food intake to bring the shortfall to zero, but not all at once. If you suddenly add back the entire shortfall, you'll gain weight because your fat cells will continue to pump calories into the bloodstream and your metabolism will remain adjusted for a lower calorie intake.

The trickiest bit is to make sure that you reintroduce the food that you didn't eat while on the diet in a gradual process. So that you don't suddenly introduce too much to soon.

The best way to do it is to add 1 to whatever you were eating. So if you were eating 1 roti, now make it 2. If you were having 2 spoons of vegetables, add another to it. If you were having 5 spoons of dahi, add one to it. This brings you out of the diet slowly without shocking your system.

With oil, start slowly. Add oil only where it's absolutely necessary. Don't go back to cooking your vegetables in a pan splashing with oil. Add one spoon only. However, by now you've learnt to cook without oil, so why not make that a habit for life?

Also, try to keep eating fruit every 30 minutes for a few weeks after you come out of your diet. This is to make sure that your stomach stays full and doesn't go into hunger mode. If you keep it empty, you might suddenly have major hunger attacks and crave junk food, which will completely throw you off balance.

Increasing the Time for Dinner

Although my mantra for staying thin is to make sure that you have a light and early dinner, I also know that many people can't work an early dinner into their routines. I always tell my clients that while on the diet that they should try to stick to the time as much as possible! But after the diet, you can shift the hour of eating dinner by 30 to 90 minutes. No more than that.

One-Week Maintenance Diet Plan

Day 1	Time	Food
	On rising: 7 and 7.30 am	Aloe vera juice (dilute half tsp of juice in half glass water) Or Lemon squeezed in hot water Or Green tea/regular tea (2 tsp skimmed milk, no sugar) Or

Day 1	Time	Food
		½ tsp methi dana (soaked overnight) + ½ tsp of flax, sunflower, and pumpkin seeds + 5 almonds (soaked overnight)
	Breakfast between 8.30 and 9.30 am	150 ml of skimmed milk + 50 g muesli Or 50 g oat flakes/50 g wheat bran
	10 and 10.30 am	1 seasonal fruit
	11 and 11.30 am	1 green vegetable salad with mixed sprouts
	Lunch between 12.30 and 1 pm	1 multigrain atta roti + 1 cup seasonal vegetable (less oil) + 1 cup yoghurt (made from skimmed milk)
	2.30 and 3 pm	½ small fruit
	Snack between 4 and 4.30 pm	Green tea/regular tea Or Coconut water + A handful of roasted puffed wheat + Roasted channas + Peanuts (total 1 small cup)

Day 1	Time	Food
	Dinner between 6.30 and 7.30 pm	Clear vegetable soup or salad + 2 egg whites scrambled with vegetables Or 60 g to 70 g tofu + Steamed veggies

Day 2	Time	Food
	On rising: 7 and 7.30 am	Same as Day 1 + Green tea/regular tea (2 tsp skimmed milk, no sugar) + 3 almonds and 1 walnut (soaked overnight)
	Breakfast between 8.30 and 9.30 am	1 oatmeal with hung curd/low-fat cheese + Fresh coconut water Or 200 ml soya milk + Vegetable sandwich (2 slices toasted)
	10 and 10.30 am	1 seasonal fruit
	11 and 11.30 am	Fresh salad with yoghurt or with 30 g tofu

Day 2	Time	Food
	Lunch between 12.30 and 1 pm	1 multigrain atta roti + 1 cup seasonal vegetable (less oil) + ½ cup daal
	2.30 and 3 pm	½ seasonal fruit
	Snack between 4 and 4.30 pm	Yakult probiotic drink + Figs + 3 almonds + 8 to 10 peanuts
	Dinner between 6.30 and 7.30 pm	Grilled chicken salad with vinegerate dressing (made with ½ lemon + ½ tsp of olive oil)

Day 3	Time	Food
	On rising: 7 and 7.30 am	Lemon water with honey (½ lemon + ¼ tsp of honey + 1 glass warm water) + Mix of flax, sesame, sunflower, water melon and pumpkin seeds (½ tsp) Or Green tea/regular tea (2 tsp skimmed milk, no sugar) + ½ walnut + 2 prunes (soaked overnight)

Day 3	Time	Food
	Breakfast between 8.30 and 9.30 am	½ cup yoghurt (made from skimmed milk) Or 1 banana smoothie + 1 apple
	10 and 10.30 am	½ seasonal fruit/roasted channa (1tbsp)
	11 and 11.30 am	Vegetable salad with homemade cottage cheese (made with 250 ml double toned milk)
	Lunch between 12.30 and 1 pm	1 barley + oat flour+ oat bran roti (equal proportions) + ½ cup yoghurt (made from skimmed milk)
	2.30 and 3 pm	Fruit (½ orange/sweet lime)
	Snack between 4 and 4.30 pm	Coconut water/cucumber + celery juice + ½ boiled potato with skin chaat Or 2 high fibre oat cookies
	Dinner between 6.30 and 7.30 pm	Mixed vegetable stew + 2 boiled egg whites

Day 4	Time	Food
	On rising: 7 and 7.30 am	Same as Day 3
	Breakfast between 8.30 and 9.30 am	1 ragi bread toast + 1 egg white omlette with vegetables Or 1 full boiled egg Or 1 Besan ka chilla with very little oil + ½ cup yoghurt or green chutney
	10 and 10.30 am	½ fruit Or 1 Yakult probiotic drink
	11 and 11.30 am	1 quarter plate raw veggie salad
	Lunch between 12.30 and 1 pm	1 brown or red rice vegetable pulao with 4 to 5 nutri-nuggets + 1 cup vegetable raita (made from skimmed milk) Or 1 stuffed vegetable ragi roti + 5 to 6 nutri nuggets with vegetables
	2.30 and 3 pm	½ seasonal fruit

Day 4	Time	Food
	Snack between 4 and 4.30 pm	1 homemade oatmeal muffin with nuts or 1 light Granola bar (not more than 70–85 calories)
	Dinner between 6.30 and 7.30 pm	300 ml of clear vegetable soup + Steamed vegetables Or 100 gm steamed white fish or paneer

Day 5	Time	Food
	On rising: 7 and 7.30 am	Tulsi + jeera+ ajwain+ methi dana + warm water + ¼ tsp mix of flax, sunflower and pumpkin seeds + 3 almonds + ½ walnut (soaked overnight)
	Breakfast between 8.30 and 9.30 am	2 multigrain toast + vegetable patty Or 250 gm brown rice poha with mixed vegetables + Coconut water

Day 5	Time	Food
	10 and 10.30 am	Fresh homemade lassi (½ cup yoghurt) Or Fruit
	11 and 11.30 am	Salad topped with roasted cashews (2) and raisins (5)
	Lunch between 12.30 and 1 pm	Dalia + dal ki khichdi (total 250 gm) + 1 cup yoghurt (made from skimmed milk) Or 1 whole wheat and wheat bran stuffed roti with vegetables + 1 cup daal
	2.30 and 3 pm	½ seasonal fruit
	Snack between 4 and 4.30 pm	Iced tea or lemon water or gingerate + 1 quarter plate roasted bhel puri Or 2 fingers of Kit-Kat chocolate
	Dinner between 6.30 and 7.30 pm	300 ml of clear vegetable soup + ½ breast of chicken salad + 2 tbsp of mixed sprouts salad

Day 6	Time	Food
	On rising: 7 and 7.30 am	Aloe vera juice (dilute half tsp of juice in half glass water + ¼ tsp mix of flax, sunflower and pumpkin seeds Or Green tea/regular tea (2 tsp skimmed milk, no sugar) + ¼ methi dana (soaked overnight)
	Breakfast between 8.30 and 9.30 am	2 multigrain toasts + 1 boiled egg white Or 150 ml milk + 1 bowl of oats
	10 and 10.30 am	½ fruit
	11 and 11.30 am	Vegetable sandwich
	Lunch between 12.30 and 1 pm	1 ragi atta + oat flour + oat bran roti (equal proportions) + 1 cup vegetables (less oil) + ½ cup yoghurt (made from skimmed milk)
	2.30 and 3 pm	½ seasonal fruit

Day 6	Time	Food
	Snack between 4 and 4.30 pm	2 multigrain crackers Or 1 banana smoothie
	Dinner between 6.30 and 7.30 pm	100 gm steamed white fish or paneer Or Steamed veggies + 2 multigrain toasts

Day 7	Time	Food
	On rising: 7 and 7.30 am	Lemon water with honey (½ lemon + ¼ tsp honey + 1 glass warm water) + Mix of flax, watermelon, sunflower, and pumpkin seeds + ½ walnut + 2 prunes (soaked overnight)
	Breakfast between 8.30 and 9.30 am	2 oatmeal toasts + 2 scrambled egg whites Or 150 ml milk + 1 bowl of oats
	10 and 10.30 am	½ seasonal fruit

Day 7	Time	Food
	11 and 11:30 am	Vegetable salad with homemade cottage cheese (made with 250 ml of double toned milk)
	Lunch between 12.30 and 1 pm	Brown or red rice pulao with vegetables + ½ cup yoghurt (made from skimmed milk)
	2.30 and 3 pm	1 citrus fruit
	Snack between 4 and 4.30 pm	Coconut water + 2 multigrain crackers
	Dinner between 6.30 and 7.30 pm	Mixed vegetable stew + 2 boiled egg whites

Exercising to Maintain Weight

If you're thinking that reaching your goal weight means you can finally slack off when it comes to exercise, then it's time to alter your mindset right now. The fact is that people who are successful at maintaining their weight over time do as much, or more, physical activity they did while losing weight. Going 'off' your diet or exercise plan, and back to the patterns that made you overweight to begin with, is a one-way ticket right back to where you started.

You don't have to make any big changes in your exercise routine at this point. In fact, the fewer changes you make, and the smaller they are, the more successful you'll be at keeping the weight off. But you will probably need to make some minor changes to stabilize your weight. Remember that exercising for weight management is not all about the big calorie burns you get from an intense workout session—it's also about walking a few extra steps every time you can, taking the stairs instead of the elevator, walking up the hill instead of going around it, sitting on a stability ball instead of a chair, doing things the old fashioned way, or pumping out a few jumping jacks during those TV commercials.

Exercising to maintain your weight isn't much different from working out to lose weight, get fit or stay fit. The important thing is that you don't slack off on any element of your exercise plan. People who struggle with their weight usually have metabolisms that naturally want to store extra energy as fat instead of burning it off. That's not going to change just because you lost weight. You'll have to work out just as hard—and as smart—to keep your metabolism in high gear and keep the weight off. Make sure that, at minimum, your exercise programme for maintenance includes these three elements:

- at least 1 hour of moderate intensity cardio, every day;
- at least two strength training sessions each week; and
- as much extra 'lifestyle activity' such as walking to the store, taking the stairs, etc., as you can manage.

Conclusion

Take a look at a scar on your body, and think back to the fall that gave you this tiny token. The pain of the fall must have been terrible and there must have been blood involved. However, now you can't feel that pain anymore, can you? All you have is a mark, which, if it wasn't a bad fall, too, will disappear in time, leaving behind no trace of the fact that you had hurt yourself.

The human body is truly wonderful and we are blessed to human which is God's miracle creation. It gives you chance after chance to heal, break a habit, grow, recover, and nourish. And yet we abuse that chance it gives us and instead indulge, indulge, indulge in pleasures which end up harming us. The body is what sustains us and if we ignore it or disregard it, it will decay and give up on us.

My mission in writing this book is to share the

message that you can get results and be fabulous if you really want it. And the best part is that it doesn't cost anything—just a strong will power and a happy disposition.

You can be successful in your career, soar the skies, if you work hard for it; you can have the happiest marriage, if you constantly work on it; and you can have the body of your dreams if you work hard for it. Eat right and party hard, and still be thin. What I've mostly said in this book isn't rocket science. We all know it, but most of us choose to ignore it or are too lazy to implement it in our lives. If you get the format of eating right, there's no way you'll ever be fat.

Believe me, over the many years of being a fitness and nutrition expert, I've seen so many successful cases that I knew for a fact that you too can achieve your goal—no matter how difficult it seems. Every time a client comes back to visit me, looking fit and gorgeous, it makes me wonder in amazement about the beauty of the human body. It's science at it's complicated and glorious best, and we're lucky to have it. So accept the gift, love it, nourish it, and most importantly stay happy and fit.

Acknowledgements

I am grateful to several people in my life who have made my work and this book possible. As a juvenile diabetic, I have faced severe medical issues and challenges, which have affected my day to day functioning. My health has deteriorated steadily—this has made me learn and understand the importance of diet and exercise and how it relates to overall health and well-being. I have also learnt the medical aspects involved in a weight loss programme. As I am dealing with my own health issues, I am constantly looking to learn and grow and try and keep abreast of new developments in diet, health, and weight loss.

In going through my health challenges, my father Dr Ashok Grover has been my guide, mentor, and supporter. My father has learnt about my medical problems and guided me in how to best deal with them. Being a doctor, he has been able to provide me with a much better insight of my client's health issues and this has, in turn, helped me to deal with them and guide them appropriately with their weight loss issues.

I would also like to thank my mother Uma Grover; her untiring and selfless support has made it possible for me to devote my efforts to my work. My mother has been a source of silent strength and as I have faced challenges in dealing with my diet issues my mother has helped me experiment on how to prepare low calorie healthy foods that are pleasing to the palate.

Both my parents have supported and encouraged me to work and given me the freedom to persue whatever would make me happy. I am eternally grateful to them for this.

A special thanks to my sister Neelima and her daughter Saachi—their positive energy and support has motivated me and encouraged me to look at food and diet from a child's perspective and experiment with recipes for children.

Thank you to my brother and sister-in-law Varun and Anita for supporting and encouraging me. A special thanks to my cousin Madhu and her husband Dr Salil Mangi for always being there for me when I have needed them to deal with my health problems. Thanks to my cousin Dr Gautam Kumar for helping me deal with my eye problems and my cousin and sister-in-law Neeto and Rita for their love, affection, and support. Also a big thanks to my friends—Antara, Humaira, Meetu, and Dipali for their love and friendship and for being there for me.

I also want to extend a special thanks to Dr Vasudeva with whom I have worked for over twenty-five years. I want to thank her for believing in me and for supporting me as I have worked with her and brought in many new ideas and changes.

Thank you to my staff. Especially Usha, Anu, Kathy, and Anna, and my café staff Sheila and Kiran for working with me over the years and supporting all my efforts.

Finally, thank you to my clients for believing in me and giving me the opportunity to help you and work with you. Thank you for your love and affection. From you I have learned the most.

A Note on the Author

Nishi Grover is a dietician, who has had over 1500 clients till now. She started as an aerobics trainer in 1988, and today charts out personalized diet plans (a combination of diet, exercise, and weight-loss therapies) for her clients. She also has a low-cal café where her clients can gorge on goodies like apple tart, kulfi, shahi tukda, and chocolate cakes—made without oil or sugar. This is her first book.